MW00389187

Best Hiking
in Southwestern Colorado
around Ouray, Telluride, Silverton
and Lake City

Diane Greer

Boot Jockey Press

Best Hiking in Southwestern Colorado around Ouray, Telluride, Silverton and Lake City

1st Edition, February 2017
ISBN: 978-0-9974780-2-0

All photos and original maps by the author
Cover photo: Blue Lakes and Blue Lakes Pass (Hike 1)

Your Safety is Your Responsibility

The author assumes no responsibility for the safety of users of this guide. Outdoor recreational activities involve a certain degree of risk and are by their very nature potentially hazardous. It is not within the scope of this guide to allow for disclosure of all potential hazards and risks involved in outdoor activities. All participants in such activities must assume the responsibility of their own actions and safety.

Furthermore, the author has done her best to make sure the information in this guide is as accurate and useful as possible. However, things can change, trails get rerouted, road conditions change, regulations are modified, etc. Hikers using the information in this guide should make allowances for the possibility that it may not be correct.

Even the best guide and maps can't replace good judgment and common sense. Be prepared and cautious. You will have a safer and more enjoyable trip.

Table of Contents

Introduction

The Basecamps

Locator Map

Ouray Hikes

Silverton Hikes

Telluride Hikes

Lake City Hikes

Appendix

Best Day Hikes in Southwest Colorado around the towns of Ouray, Telluride, Silverton and Lake City

An opinionated guide to the best day hikes in one of Colorado's best hiking areas, the western San Juan Mountains

If you're like me you love to hike and want to spend as much of your vacation and time off as possible on the trail. The challenge is weeding through all the online and hardcopy information to find the best hikes -- the trails that take you above timberline to beautiful mountain lakes nestled in dramatic cirques, to passes with see forever views and to glorious alpine meadows filled with wildflowers.

This opinionated guide does the work for you, choosing the best day hikes in one of Colorado's best hiking areas, the western San Juan Mountains around the towns of Ouray, Telluride, Silverton and Lake City. The San Juans, the largest mountain range in Colorado, encompasses more than 10,000 square-miles of some of the most spectacular peaks, ridges and glacial valleys in the state. Sixteen peaks tower above 14,000-ft. and hundreds top 13,000-ft. Three national forests and seven wilderness areas protect huge swathes of this amazing landscape.

The trails in this guide, best hiked between mid-July and mid-September, appeal to day hikers who like to go high and walk 6.0 to 12.5 miles/day. Elevation gains range from 1,000 to 3,500-ft. Many of the trails offer great intermediate turnaround points for those seeking shorter hikes. All are reached in less than an hour drive from four great base camps; Ouray, Telluride, Silverton and Lake City.

Ouray, Telluride and Silverton are beautifully preserved Victorian era mining towns, each with its own distinct personality. The towns are linked by the stunning San Juan Skyway scenic drive, a 233-mile loop traversing the heart of the San Juan Mountains, which also passes through Durango, Cortez and numerous historic sites.

A little further afield is Lake City, a small, remote Victorian town linked with Ouray and Silverton by the Alpine Loop National Backcountry Byway, a network of jeep roads traversing stunning scenery, visiting ghost towns and crossing passes up to 12,800-ft. Visitors driving passenger cars reach the idyllic little hamlet along Highway 149, aka the Silver Thread Scenic Byway, a road with some really beautiful scenery and a good dose of history.

Each town offers accommodations, campgrounds, restaurants and bars catering to all budget levels. Groceries, outdoor stores and laundromats along with bakeries and internet cafes provide the essential services needed by outdoor travelers.

The first section of this guide describes the towns, identifying local services, highlighting nearby attractions and suggesting activities for nonhiking/rainy days. The second section offers detailed trail descriptions with photos, maps and elevation profiles of the recommended hikes.

Extensive photo galleries and interactive maps with GPS tracks of the hikes are available on a companion website – www.hikingwalking.com.

I love feedback and would like to hear your opinion on how to improve the guide and the website. Obviously the selection of the best hikes is subjective, based on my personal opinion. Send an email (editor@hikingwalking.com) or post a comment on the website about the pros and cons of a particular hike or if you believe other hikes should be included in the "best of" list.

About the Ratings

All the hikes in this guide are recommended. That being said I want to make it easier for hikers to differentiate between trails. As such, hikes within a region are rated in relation to other hikes in the area. That does not mean that a hike rated as three stars is not worth doing. It just means if you only have a few days in a given area you might want to consider tackling the higher rated hikes first.

Abbreviations

RT – Round-Trip, NF – National

Ouray, Colorado

Location: On Highway 550, 35 miles south of Montrose, CO and 70 miles north of Durango, CO.

Ouray (7,746-ft.) is a pretty little Victorian mountain town nestled beneath a dramatic granite amphitheater and surrounded by 12,000-ft. plus peaks. A variety of accommodations and services along with its close proximity to some of the regions great hikes makes the town a perfect base camp for outdoor enthusiasts.

The town is located in the heart of the Uncompahgre National Forest in southwest Colorado, 35 miles south of Montrose and 70 miles north of Durango, CO on Highway 550. Distinctive Mt. Sneffels (14,150-ft.), rising to the west of town, is the center piece of the 16,500-acre Mt. Sneffels Wilderness. Northeast of Ouray is the 99,000-acre Uncompahgre Wilderness, home to two fourteeners, Wetterhorn Peak (14,015-ft.) and Uncompahgre Peak (14,309-ft.) along with numerous peaks over 13,000-ft.

Around Town

During the day Ouray (pronounced "you-ray" by the locals) is a popular stop for sightseers driving the San Juan Skyway, a stunning 233-mile loop that crosses four high passes and connects Ouray to Silverton, Durango, Cortez, and Telluride (going clockwise around the loop). The Skyway's steady stream of tourists helps support a good selection of restaurants, bars and breweries along with a range of accommodations that includes condos, cabins and home vacations rentals, B&B's, hotels/motels and campground/RV parks.

By 4pm the day trippers plying the scenic byways disappear and the town takes on a more laid back, family atmosphere. Be sure to spend at least one of your evenings strolling Ouray's back streets admiring the beautifully restored Victorian architecture. The entire town is listed on the National Register of Historic Districts and most of its structures, built between 1880 and 1900 during the area's mining boom, are still standing.

My favorite place in town is Ouray's Hot Springs. After a hard day of hiking nothing is better than soaking in the pools fed by natural hot springs while admiring the red sandstone and granite cliffs towering above town. The facility is configured into different pools ranging in temperature from 96-105 degrees and includes a cooler lap swimming section, diving area and kiddie wading pool. The adjacent park is a nice place for a picnic. Ouray Tourism is located next to the facility.

A short walk in town to the end of east 8th Avenue will take you to the base of Cascade Falls, the lowest segment of a series of seven waterfalls draining snowmelt from the peaks above town. Box Canon Waterfalls and Park, located on CR 361 off Highway 550 just south of Ouray, is an interesting geological formation featuring a 285-ft. waterfall plummeting through a narrow box canyon. It is worth the entrance fee and the hour or so spent viewing the formation and walking the three interpretive trails. Another nice walk is the Uncompahgre River trail on the west side of town, which starts on the west side of town just north of the Hot Springs and meanders along the river to Ouray's northern border.

The Ouray Perimeter trail is a good option for visitors looking for a longer walk. The 5.0 miles trail, which can be accessed from several spots around town, visits Cascade Falls, the Baby Bathtubs and crosses over Canon Creek's spectacular gorge. Along the way enjoy great views of Mt. Abrams, Hayden Mountain, Whitehouse Mountain, Twin Peaks and the Amphitheater. An optional detour includes a visit to Box Canyon Park. A map and additional information about the Perimeter Trail is available at the Ouray Visitor Center.

Nearby Attractions

There is plenty to do around Ouray if you decide to take a day off from hiking. Most people drive the Million Dollar Highway, the 24 miles section of the San Juan Skyway between Ouray and Silverton. The route traverses jaw dropping scenery littered with mining relics and climbs over 11,018-ft Red Mountain Pass. A full day needs to be allocated to drive the entire San Juan Skyway. This trip is better done as part of an extended trip with overnight stops in Silverton and Telluride.

Another interesting diversion is a trip to one of the area's ghost towns. A few are accessible with a passenger vehicle but most require a 4WD (tours are available). The Ouray Visitor Center located by the Hot Springs has a complete list of the options along with directions and recommendations.

Those with a 4WD and taste for adventure may want to drive the area's famous backcountry roads. Yankee Boy Basin, to the southwest of town, provides opportunities to visit several ghost towns, view beautiful Twin Falls and, during late July/early August, see spectacular displays of wildflowers. The Alpine Loop is another popular route leading over 12,000-ft passes to the Lake City and back. Be sure to check with the local tourism office about road conditions and the skill level required to drive each of the routes.

A tour of the Bachelors Syracuse Mine is a good option for a rainy day. (See also Old Hundred Gold Mine Tour outside of Silverton.) A guide with experience working the mine takes visitors 1,800 feet horizontally into Gold Hill to a work area used to extract the silver and other minerals. The tour includes a complete presentation of the equipment and techniques used to extract the ore.

Food, Lodging and Services

Just about all the basic services you need are found along Main Street, a six block section of Highway 550 running through the center of town. The Ouray Visitor Center, open 7 days a week during the summer, is located at 1230 Main Street, next to the Hot Springs Pool.

Duckett's Market, a small grocery at 621 Main Street, offers the basics for making a meal. Those looking for the wider selection should travel 11 miles north to the Ridgway Mountain Market (490 Sherman St, Ridgway) or purchase groceries in Montrose or Durango. Coffee and internet fixes along with baked goods and sandwiches are available at Back Street Bistro coffee shop (219 Seventh Avenue). Ouray Mountain Sports (732 Main St.) stocks clothing and gear for climbers and hikers. A surprisingly good selection of maps, guides and leisure reading material can be found at Buckskin Booksellers at 505 Main St.

Resources and Links

Ouray Visitor Center - www.ouraycolorado.com – 1230 Main Street

Uncompahgre National Forest - Ouray District Office, 2505 S. Townsend, Montrose, CO 81401, 970-240-5300 - www.fs.usda.gov/gmug

Ouray Trails Group - Short descriptions of area trails - http://www.ouraytrails.org/

(Short trail descriptions are also available from the Ouray Information Center - www.ouraycolorado.com/things-to-do/hiking)

Food, Lodging and Retail

Ouray Mountain Sports - ouraysports.com/ - 732 Main St.

Buckskin Booksellers - www.buckskinbooksellers.com/ - 505 Main Street

Duckett's Market - www.ouraycolorado.com/directory/shopping-retail/shops/107-duckett-s-a-g-market - 621 Main Street

Ridgway Mountain Market - ridgwaymountainmarket.com/, 490 Sherman St, Ridgway, CO, (11 miles north of Ouray.

Backstreet Bistro - www.ouraycolorado.com/directory/dining-nightlife/restaurants-in-ouray/35-backstreet-bistro, 219 Seventh Avenue

Accommodations - Condos, cabins and home vacations rentals, B&B's, hotels/motels and campground/RV parks listings from Ouray Tourism - www.ouraycolorado.com/directory/lodging-camping

Campgrounds and RV Parks

U.S. Forest Service: Amphitheater Campground - is located on the side of a mountain above the east side of Ouray, Colorado at an elevation of about 8,400 ft. It is tightly designed with loops and camping spurs among Gamble oaks and mixed conifers. There is a scenic overlook in the campground with views of Ouray and the "Amphitheater," which was formed by a volcanic explosion. Firewood is available for a fee. The campground is best suited for tents, but RVers can utilize sites 3 through 15.

Total RV length should not exceed 35 feet.
(www.fs.usda.gov/recarea/gmug/recarea/?recid=32522)

Ridgway State Park Campground - This is a full-service facility with 258 RV/tent sites, 25 walk in tent sites and 3 Yurts. The campground is located in 15 miles north of Ouray in Ridgway State Park, a facility that includes a beautiful reservoir, picnic and playground areas and trail system. Fees apply. www.parks.state.co.us/Parks/Ridgway/Pages/RidgwayStateParkHome.aspx

Private Campground – 4J+1+1 RV Campground - 790 Oak Street, Ouray

Tours and Attractions

Bachelors Syracuse Mine Tour - http://www.bachelorsyracusemine.com/ - 1222 County Road 14, Ouray, CO
Box Canyon Falls - http://www.ouraycolorado.com/listing/boxcanyon

Silverton, Colorado

Location: On Highway 550, 23 miles south of Ouray and 50 miles north of Durango.

Silverton (9,318-ft.) is a wonderfully preserved mining town set in a high mountain valley surrounded by 13,000-ft. peaks. Primarily constructed between 1882 and 1910, the entire town is a national historic landmark and considered one of the most intact sites of its kind in the country.

Silverton is a little grittier and rougher around the edges then nearby Ouray. What the town lacks in polish it makes up for with location, surrounded by BLM land and three national forests featuring stunning alpine valleys, emerald green meadows and towering peaks. The Weminuche Wilderness, the State's largest, is located southeast of town. The Continental Divide and the Colorado Trails traverse the high country to the south and east.

Getting to Silverton is its own adventure. The town lies sandwiched between high passes on Highway 550, aka the Million Dollar Highway, 23 miles south of Ouray and 50 miles north of Durango. Driving south from Ouray on 550, the narrow, winding highway ascends through fabulous scenery littered with mining ruins to cross Red Mountain Pass (11,018-ft.) before dropping to Silverton. The route north from Durango is just as spectacular, crossing Coal Bank (10,640-ft.) and Molas (10,970-ft.) passes along the way.

Around Town

During Silverton's heyday in the 1880's, millions of dollars in gold and silver extracted from nearby mines fueled construction of lavish hotels and ornate homes, occupied by the town's law-abiding and respectable citizens, along with dance halls, brothels and saloons frequented by a rougher crowd.

10

Because Silverton never experienced a major fire a good number of these buildings are still standing.

Today the town boasts of its dual personalities, the respectable half west of Greene Street (the town's main drag) and the "red light district" east of Greene around notorious Blair Street, once home to over 40 saloons and brothels. Many of the restored structures on Greene, Blair and the adjacent side streets are now eclectic gift shops and restaurants catering to tourist.

Tourism is the mainstay of Silverton's economy. During the summer and early fall the Durango and Silverton Narrow Gauge Railroad (D&SNG) makes the 45-mile run between Durango and Silverton several times a day, bringing an influx of tourists who spend a few hours sightseeing, shopping and eating before returning to Durango.

The town is also is a popular stop for sightseers driving the San Juan Skyway, a 233-mile loop with stunning scenery that crosses four high passes and connects Silverton to Ouray, Telluride, Cortez, and Durango (going clockwise around the loop).

By late afternoon most of the train tourists are gone and the town takes on a more relaxed and authentic atmosphere. The evenings are a good time to stroll the streets and appreciate the historic buildings. Take time to tour the backstreets west of Greene to see beautifully restored Victorian homes along with buildings undergoing restoration.

For a bird's eye view of Silverton and the surrounding area take an evening stroll to the Christ of the Mine Shrine, a huge statue of Jesus in a stone alcove located 500 feet up the slope of Anvil Mountain north of Silverton. Reach the shrine by walking northwest on 10th Street to its end at Keystone Street where an obvious trail ascends the hillside to the statue.

The San Juan County Museum, located in the old San Juan County Jail at the northeast end of Green Street, is worth a visit and a good rainy day diversion. The museum features artifacts and displays explaining the history of the town, the area's mining legacy and the D&SNG railroad.

Nearby Attractions

When you need a break from hiking visit Animas Forks, a ghost town located 15 miles northeast of Silverton on County Road 2, is an interesting option. A surprising number of buildings and mining structure still stand at the site, inhabited from the 1870's to the 1920's. BLM plaques describe the structures and the history of the town. The dirt road leading to the site is accessible to passenger vehicles.

Another good diversion is the drive to Ouray along the 24-mile stretch of Highway 550 dubbed the Million Dollar Highway. The drive features incredible mountain scenery, deep canyons, sheer cliffs and numerous mining ruins. Ouray (7,746-ft.) is a pretty little Victorian town nestled beneath a dramatic granite amphitheater and surrounded by 12,000-ft. plus peaks. See the Ouray section of the guide for more information.

A tour of the Old Hundred Mine is a great option for a rainy day. To reach the mine travel 4 miles northeast from Silverton on County Road 2. Turn right onto Country Road 4A and follow the signs for 0.75 miles to the mine. The tour takes visitors 1,500-ft into a gold mine for demonstrations of mining equipment and operations.

Self-guided tours are available at the Mayflower Gold Mill, a National Historic Landmark located 2 miles northeast of Silverton on County Road 2. The tour explains the operation of the largely intact Mill that processed gold and silver for almost a half century.

Hikers with a 4WD vehicle or a mountain bike might want to investigate the old mining roads crisscrossing the backcountry around Silverton. Many lead to ghost towns, mining ruins and spectacular vistas. Be sure to check at the Silverton Visitor Center (414 Greene Street) regarding road conditions and the skill level required to navigate the roads. Jeep rentals and 4WD tours of the backcountry are offered by various businesses in town.

The Alpine Loop, a National Backcountry Byway, is the area's most popular backcountry adventure. From Silverton the 65-mile 4WD route starts at the ghost town at Animas Forks, climbs over Cinnamon Pass (12,620-ft.) and drops down to Lake City on Highway 149. From the south end of Lake City the return route follows the Henson Creek drainage to Engineer Pass (12,800-ft.) and then drops back down to Animas Forks. Along the way the route traverses beautiful mountain landscapes with panoramic vistas and passes historic ghost towns and mining sites.

Food, Lodging and Services

Greene Street (the town's main drag), Blair Street and the adjacent side streets are lined with restaurants, cafes and quaint shops catering to tourist and outdoor enthusiast.

Accommodations range from B&B's and small hotels, situated in historic buildings with period furnishings, to more modern motels. A variety of homes and apartments are available as vacation rentals. Four RV Parks are located in or near town while the surrounding national forests offer established campgrounds and dispersed camping opportunities.

The tourist information center is on your right as you enter town at 414 Green Street. Silverton Grocery at 717 Greene Street stocks the basics needed to assemble a meal. Those looking for the wider selection should purchase groceries in Ridgway or Durango.

Avalanche Coffee House (1067 Blair Street) will satisfy your caffeine habit and has a good variety of baked goods, sandwiches and snacks. Outdoor World (1234 Greene Street) offers a nice selection of hiking and fishing gear along area maps and guidebooks.

Resources and Links

Silverton Visitor Information - //www.silvertoncolorado.com

Uncompahgre National Forest - //www.fs.usda.gov/gmug

San Juan National Forest - //www.fs.usda.gov/sanjuan

Food, Lodging and Retail

Silverton Grocery - Groceries, snacks, beer, video rentals. 717 Greene St.

Outdoor World – Hiking, backpacking, fishing gear along with maps and guidebooks, 1234 Greene Street

Avalanche Coffee House - Coffee and tea, fresh-baked breads and pastries, homemade light fare, gourmet pizza., 1067 Blair St.

Lodging Info - from the Silverton Chamber of Commerce - www.silvertoncolorado.com/index.php?biz=yes&bizstatus=viewcat&cat_id =8

Dining Info - from the Silverton Chamber of Commerce - www.silvertoncolorado.com/index.php?biz=yes&bizstatus=viewcat&cat_id =7

Shopping Info - from the Silverton Chamber of Commerce - www.silvertoncolorado.com/index.php?biz=yes&bizstatus=viewcat&cat_id =7

Campgrounds and RV Parks

A & B RV Park - Full hookups; 30 & 50 amp; large spaces; TV; showers; laundry. 1445 Mineral St.

Red Mountain Motel, Cabins & RV Park - 38 full hookup sites. Camp, jeep, ATV, OHV, fish, hunt; tent, snowmobile. Motel (summer only), cabins (year round); laundry. 664 Greene St. - www.redmtmotelrvpk.com

Silver Summit RV Park - 640 Mineral St., www.silversummitrvpark.com

Molas Lake Park - Camping, cabins, fishing, hiking, horseback rides & canoeing. 6 miles south of Silverton on Highway 550, Molas Lake.

South Mineral Campground – Take Highway 550 2 miles west of Silverton and turn left onto Forest Rd. 585. Follow 585 for 4.4 miles to the campground which has 26 sites. Dispersed camping sites are located along much of FR 585 between the highway and the South Mineral Campground.

Tours

Old Hundred Gold Mine Tour - 4 miles northeast of Silverton - 1-800-872-3009 or www.minetour.com

Mayflower Gold Mill Tour - 4 miles northeast of Silverton - www.sanjuancountyhistoricalsociety.org/mayflower-mill.html

Telluride, Colorado

Location: On Highway 145, 67 miles southwest of Montrose, CO, and 75 miles northeast of Cortez, CO.

Telluride (8,745-ft), Ouray's larger and classier neighbor, is tucked at the head of a stunning box canyon and surrounded by steep valley walls and peaks rising over 13,000-ft. Like Ouray, the town started as a mining camp in the late 1800's. At the turn of the century and the height of the mining boom the town had almost 5,000 residents and more millionaires per capita than New York City.

By the mid 1950's the boom had turned to bust with most of the mines shuttered and its residents gone. The opening of the Telluride Ski Resort in 1972 changed the town's fortunes. White gold, in the form of snow, transformed the town into a world-class ski resort with a full complement of accommodations, restaurants and retail establishments.

Thankfully the town planners opted to preserve the Victorian charm of the town center, now listed as a National Historic District. An expanded ski area and modern mountain village was built close to Telluride but hidden from view by the 9,000-ft. San Sophia Ridge. The town and the mountain village are linked by a free gondola.

Around Town

Visitors flock to Telluride in the summer, drawn by the area's natural beauty, diverse outdoor activities and festivals. Hikers can literally roll out of bed and walk to trailheads in town leading to some of the region's best hikes. Ten miles to the southwest lies the Lizard Head Wilderness, encompassing three fourteeners and several other summits over 13,000-ft.

If you like Victorian architecture take a stroll along the town's backstreets to see restored structures as well as recently built houses in keeping with the town's historic character. Another nice walk is the 4.25 mile San Miguel River trail, a walking and bicycle path that meanders through town along the river past the park and campground to the Pandora Mine.

Bridal Veil Falls, the tallest freefalling waterfall in Colorado, is a favorite destination located 4 miles east of Telluride. Head east on Colorado Avenue to the parking lot just past the Pandora Mine. Follow the 4WD road as it switchbacks uphill for 1.2 miles to the base of the falls. This vantage point provides great views of the waterfall plunging 365-ft. from just beneath the historic Bridal Veil power plant to a stream feeding the San Miguel River. The viewpoint is often enveloped in mist from the water thundering over the rock face and hitting a small pool at the base of the falls.

You can follow the road from the remaining 0.8 miles to a gate blocking further vehicle access up the Bridal Veil Basin. This section of the road enjoys wonderful views of the steep cliffs forming the head of the Telluride valley and the town in the distance. Along the way dramatic views open to the power plant perched atop a rock ledge just above the falls. The building, restored in the 1990's, is listed on the National Register of Historic places. For a closer view of the plant duck through the gate and follow the seldom used mining road for a few minutes to a viewpoint just above the power plant building. (The building and the area around the plant it is private property.)

A hike to Bear Creek Falls is another popular walk. The 2.3 mile trail (one-way) starts at the south end of Pine Street and follows a good trail through the 325-acre Bear Creek Preserve to a great viewpoint showcasing the falls. Total elevation gain is just over 1,380-ft. Hikers with the time and energy can continue up the dramatic Bear Creek canyon on the Wasatch trail.

Nearby Attractions

A variety of activities are available if you want to take a day off from hiking. A short scenic drive along the San Juan Skyway on Highway 45 south of Telluride leads past Trout Lake to Lizard Head Pass (10,222-ft.) where you can enjoy views of Lizard Head's distinctive lone spire rising 400-ft. above its rocky pedestal. Be sure to take a side trip to Trout Lake and the little mining town of Ophir along the way.

Driving north along the San Juan Skyway leads to Placerville, where the route turns right (east) on Highway 62 over Dallas Divide (8,983-ft.) to Ridgway. The drive between Dallas Divide and Ridgway offers panoramic views of the Mount Sneffels Range and the jagged ridges of the Uncompahgre Wilderness rising to the east.

Ridgway, a small town set in the beautiful Uncompahgre Valley, is home to a number of art galleries, antique stores and interesting retail establishments.

A full day needs to be allocated to drive the entire San Juan Skyway. At Ridgway the route turns right on U.S. 550, heading south toward Ouray and Silverton. This section of the route, which features amazing scenery littered with mining relics, climbs over 11,018-ft Red Mountain Pass on its way to Silverton. My recommendation is to drive this route as part of an extended trip with overnight stops in Ouray and Silverton. Archaeology buffs will also want to take a side trip to Mesa Verde near Cortez, to view the Anasazi cliff dwellings.

Several 4WD roads lead to ghost towns and stunning views. The easiest is the 5-mile road to Alta Lakes and Alta Ghost town. Be sure to check at the visitor center regarding road conditions and the skill level required to navigate the roads. Mountain bikers will find plenty of trails and 4WD roads of varying lengths and difficulties.

Food, Lodging and Services

Telluride features a full complement of accommodations, restaurants and shops. The town's main street, Colorado Avenue, and the adjacent side streets are lined with an eclectic collection of galleries, boutiques, specialty stores, restaurants and gift shops. Numerous outdoor stores such as the Jagged Edge Mountain Gear (223 E Colorado Ave) and Telluride Sports (150 W. Colorado) cater to climbers, hikers and fisherman.

Clark's Market at 700 W Colorado and the Village Market, at 157 Fir Street, stock just about everything you need to cook the most elaborate of meals. Baked in Telluride, at 127 Fir Street, turns out delicious goodies as well as sandwiches and snacks. Caffeine addicts can get their daily fix at Coffee Cowboy at 131 E. Colorado or at High Alpine Coffee in the back of Between the Covers Bookstore, at 224 W Colorado.

The visitor center and central reservation office is located at 236 W. Colorado Avenue. Between the Covers at 224 W Colorado is the place to got for maps, guidebooks and leisure reading material.

Resources and Links

Telluride Tourism - www.visittelluride.com/ - 700 W Colorado Avenue.

Uncompahgre National Forest - www.fs.usda.gov/gmug

San Juan National Forest - www.fs.usda.gov/sanjuan

Food, Lodging and Retail

Clark's Market - Supermarket - 700 W. Colorado Avenue - www.clarksmarket.com

Village Market, 157 S. Fir St.

Baked in Telluride - 127 S. Fir Street - www.bakedintelluride.com

Maggie's Bakery & Cafe, 300 West Colorado Avenue

Between the Covers Bookstore and Espresso Bar - 224 W. Colorado Avenue - www.between-the-covers.com

Jagged Edge - Sporting Goods, Maps and Books - 223 E. Colorado Avenue - www.jagged-edge-telluride.com

Telluride Sports - Sporting Goods, Maps and Books - 150 W. Colorado Avenue - www.telluridesports.com

Telluride Accommodations Directory - www.visittelluride.com/places-to-stay

Camping and RV Parks

Alta Lakes Campground - Take Highway 145 south for about 10 miles to the Boomerang Road, Alta Lakes. Drive 5-miles on the rough road to the campsite located a 11,200-ft. Dispersed camping, pit toilet, free. (www.fs.usda.gov/recarea/gmug/recreation/camping-cabins/recarea/?recid=34056&actid=29)

Matterhorn Campground – Located 7 miles south of Telluride on Highway 145. This campground has showers, dumping station/sewer hookups, electric hookups.
(www.fs.usda.gov/recarea/gmug/recreation/camping-cabins/recarea/?recid=32376&actid=29)

Sunshine Campground – 12 miles south of Telluride on Highway 145 on the right side of the highway. There are 18 sites, 2 wheelchair accessible compost restrooms, metal tables and fire grates at each site.
(www.fs.usda.gov/recarea/gmug/recreation/camping-cabins/recarea/?recid=32454&actid=29)

Telluride Town Park Campground – Located along the river at the east end of town. (www.visittelluride.com/accommodation/telluride-town-park-campground)

Woods Lake Campground – Travel west on Highway 145 toward Placerville for 9 miles and turn left on Fall Creek Road. Follow the road to Woods Lake. The campground offers 41 designated sites, hand pumped water and vault toilets.
(www.fs.usda.gov/recarea/gmug/recreation/camping-cabins/recarea/?recid=32380&actid=29)

List of Other Area Campgrounds - Includes both public and private campgrounds. (www.visittelluride.com/places-to-stay/rv-camping)

Lake City, Colorado

Location: On CO-149, 55 miles southwest of Gunnison and 119 miles northwest of Alamosa.

Lake City (8,663-ft.) is a remote little Victorian town situated at the confluence of the Lake Fork of the Gunnison River and Henson Creek and surrounded by the Uncompahgre and Gunnison National Forests and the Gunnison BLM district. The town is located along CO-149, 55 miles south of Gunnison and 74 miles north of South Fork.

With close to one thousand square miles of public land nearby there is no shortage of excellent hiking opportunities. Trails climb the area's five 14,000-ft. peaks, wander through wildflower-filled meadows and traverse vast expanses of alpine tundra. Since this remote corner of the state is still relatively unknown hikers can enjoy a degree of solitude not possible in other areas of the state.

Around Town

In the late 1800's Lake City served as a supply hub and smelting center for miners in the nearby San Juan Mountains. In its heyday the town saw the construction of more than 500 structures. Mining activity and the population of the town and Hinsdale County peaked around 1900. Over the next century mining activity waned and the town went through a period of decline.

Today the charming Victorian town, a designated national historic district, is a hub for outdoor enthusiasts exploring the area's stunning mountain terrain. Over 200 of Lake City's original Victorian structures, including commercial building, churches, homes, cabins and public buildings, still stand, many restored to their former glory.

Highly recommended is an evening stroll along the town's wooden sidewalks and backstreets to see the restored structures from the 1870's and 1880's. Also of interested are the nicely preserved circa 1930-1950 motor court cabins. Pamphlets mapping a self-guided tour of the historic district are available at the Hinsdale County Museum at the corner of Second and Silver Street. The museum, run by the Hinsdale County Historic Society, chronicling the area's history is also worth a visit.

For a glimpse of mining life take a tour of the Hard Tack Mine. The underground mine tour describes the tools and techniques used by hard rock miners and includes exhibits explaining local mining history and equipment along with a rock gallery showcasing the mine's huge collection of rocks and minerals. The Hard Tack is located on County Road 20 toward Engineer's Pass, just 2.5 miles outside of town.

If your dogs are tired from hiking take a drive along the Silver Thread Scenic Byway. The route heads south from Lake City on CO-149 to Windy Point, located just before Slumgullion Pass. From this vantage point panoramic views encompass four 14,000-ft. peaks, Redcloud (14,034 ft.), Sunshine (14,001 ft.), Uncompahgre Peak (14,309-ft.), and Wetterhorn (14,015-ft.), towering above the town to the northwest. Below is Lake San Cristobal and to the north the Slumgullion Earthflow, comprised of two major earthflows. The first flow occurred about 700 years ago when a huge mass of volcanic rock slumped down the valley, damming the Lake Fork of the Gunnison River and creating Lake San Cristobal. The second slide, visible from Windy Point, started 300 years ago and is still moving down the hillside. The bizarre angle of the trees growing along the hillside illustrates the continued movement of the slide.

The byway continues over Slumgullion Pass heading south to Creede, along the way passing through incredibly beautiful landscape. A few miles north of Creede is the turnoff to the Rio Grande Reservoir. The reservoir is stocked with fish and open to boats.

Creede, located near the headwaters of the Rio Grande, is a nicely preserved rustic mining town. The historic structures along the town's main drag, Historic Street, are now home to a few restaurants and shops. Beyond Creede the road parallels the Rio Grande beneath towering cliffs, ending in South Fork.

The byway also heads north from Lake City, again following CO-149 north to Blue Mesa Lake west of Gunnison.

Just two miles south of town on US-149 is the turnoff for the road leading to Lake San Cristobal. This beautiful lake is a great place for fishing, boating, kayaking and canoeing. The Red Gulch Day Use area at the south end of the lake includes picnic facilities. The county-owned Wupperman Campground is located on the east side of the lake.

Four wheel drive enthusiasts will want to check out the Alpine Loop National Backcountry Byway. The byway is composed of several jeep roads that link Lake City with Ouray and Silverton to the west. The byway's network of roads traverse stunning scenery, visit ghost towns and cross passes up to 12,880-ft. Check with the Lake City Visitor Center at 800 Gunnison Avenue for information on road conditions and technical skills required to navigate the route.

Food, Lodging and Services

For a small town Lake City has a nice selection of accommodations, restaurants and retail shops. Accommodations include B&B's, small motels, lodges and cabins in town and at Lake San Cristobal. There are also a variety of homes and apartments available as vacation rentals.

People who prefer camping will find five campgrounds in the Uncompahgre and Gunnison National Forests near Lake City. There is also the county-owned Wupperman Campground at Lake San Cristobal, located on the east side of the lake. A list of the other public camping facilities can be found here. There are also a number of private campgrounds and RV parks in the area.

Your first stop in town should be the Visitor Center on 800 Gunnison Avenue, where you can pick up a map, learn about current conditions and get advice on recreation activities and nearby attractions. For groceries visit the Country Store Grocery at 916 N State Highway 149, which carries the basics needed to assemble a meal, and the Country Grocery Store at 916 N State Highway 149.

A wonderful selection of baked goods and fresh bread is available at the Lake City Bakery, at 922 N Highway 149. The Chillin Internet Coffee Shope and Cafe is the best place in town for a caffeine injection. For a complete list of local retail shops and services visit the Lake City Chamber of Commerce.

Resources and Links

Lake City Visitor Center - 800 Gunnison Avenue, Lake City, CO, http://www.lakecity.com

Grand Mesa, Uncompahgre and Gunnison National Forest - Near district office: Gunnison District Office at 216 N. Colorado, Gunnison, CO, 970-641-0471, www.fs.usda.gov/main/gmug/home

Short Trail Descriptions from the Lake City Visitor Center, www.lakecity.com/mountain-town-activities/24-things-to-do/trails

Trail and Road Conditions - provided by the Lake City Visitor Center, www.lakecity.com/plan-your-colorado-trip/trail-road-conditions

Food, Lodging and Retail

Lake City Accommodations and Campgrounds - www.lakecity.com/business-directory/2-accommodations

High Country Market - located at 130 Gunnison Avenue in Lake City, www.thehighcountrymarket.com/

Country Grocery Store - located at 916 N State Highway 149 in Lake City.

Lake City Bakery - 922 N Highway 149, recommended for pastries, breads and other goodies. Good place to stop for coffee, breakfast and lunch items.

Chillin Internet Coffee Shope and Cafe – 205 Gunnison Ave., Great place to satisfy your caffeine addiction. Also severs breakfast and lunch.

The General Store - located at 252 S Gunnison Ave in Lake City stocks housewares, hardware, camping and fishing supplies, books and more.

Tours and Attractions

Hardtack Mine Tour - This underground mine tour describes the tools and techniques used by hard rock miners and includes exhibits explaining local mining history and equipment along with a rock gallery showcasing the mine's huge collection of rocks and minerals. http://hardtackmine.com/

Hinsdale County Museum -Nice local museum with displays chronicling the area history. www.lakecitymuseum.com/

Silverthread Scenic Byway - Head south on Highway 149 to see the Slumgullion Earth Slide and take in the views from Slumgullion Pass. Take a side trip to Lake San Cristobal, the Rio Grand Reservoir and the historic town of Creede. www.codot.gov/programs/aeronautics/travel/scenic-byways/south-central/silver-thread

Last Chance Mine - See the ruins of the old mine and collect rock specimens. www.lastchancemine.com

Creede Underground Mining Museum - Retired miners lead tours of a closed mine, explaining the equipment and methods used to extract minerals. www.undergroundminingmuseum.com/mining-museum.html .

Wheeler Geologic Area - An amazing area of eroded outcroppings of volcanic ash in the La Garita Mountains northeast of Creede. Arrange to see this geologic wonder with a local jeep tour operator or backpack into the area on one of several trails in the Rio Grande National Forest. en.wikipedia.org/wiki/Wheeler_Geologic_Area

List of Hikes and Locator Maps

Hikes with distances and difficulty rating

Ouray Hikes

1. Blue Lakes/Blue Lakes Pass: 6.3-11 miles (RT), moderate-strenuous
2. Bridge of Heaven: 8 miles (RT), strenuous
3. Bear Creek: 4.4-8.0 miles (RT), moderate
4. Wetterhorn Basin: 5.8-9 miles (RT), moderate
5. Blaine Basin: 6.8 miles (RT), moderate
6. Upper Cascade Falls: 4.4-5.9 miles (RT), moderate-strenuous
7. Portland: 3.5 miles (RT), easy
8. Alpine Mine Overlook: 5.6 miles (RT), moderate-strenuous

Silverton Hikes

9. Ice Lakes: 7.0-8.2 miles (RT), moderate-strenuous
10. Columbine Lake/Pass: 7.0-8.9 miles (RT), moderate-strenuous
11. Porphyry Basin: 5.0 - 7.0 miles (RT), moderate
12. Highland Mary Lakes: 6.6-7.8 miles (RT), moderate-strenuous
13. Crater Lakes: 11 miles (RT), easy-moderate
14. Colorado Trail: Little Molas Lake to Lime Creek: 7.4-10.1 miles (RT), easy-moderate

Telluride Hikes

15. Sneffels Highline: 8.0-12.7 mile loop, strenuous
16. Lewis Lake and Mine: 8.0-8.8 miles (RT), moderate-strenuous
17. Blue Lake in Bridal Veil Basin: 6.0 miles (RT), moderate
18. Bridal Veil Falls: 4.0 miles (RT), moderate
19. See Forever/Wasatch/Bear Creek Loop: 5.0-8.4 mile loop, strenuous
20. Wasatch: 12.3 miles (RT), strenuous
21. Bear Creek Falls: 4.6 miles (RT), easy-moderate
22. Lake Hope: 4.5-5.9 miles (RT), moderate
23. Lizard Head: 7.6-11.7 mile loop, strenuous
24. Cross Mountain: 6.6 miles (RT), moderate-strenuous
25. Old Railroad Grade: 2.3 miles one way, easy
26. Navajo Lake: 9.2 miles (RT), moderate-strenuous
27. Kilpacker Trail to Navajo Lake: 11.8 miles (RT), moderate-strenuous

See Map on the Next Page

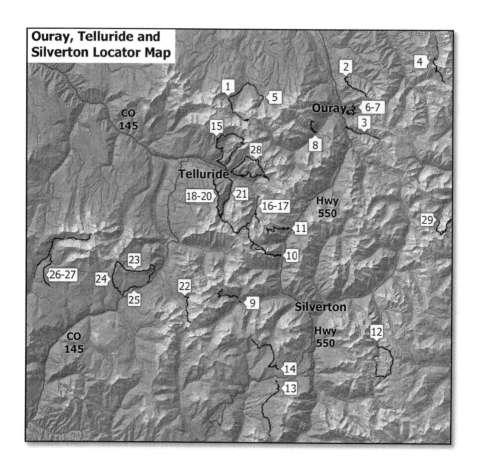

Ouray, Telluride and Silverton Locator Map

CO 145

Ouray

Telluride

Hwy 550

Silverton

Hwy 550

CO 145

Lake City Hikes

29. Handies Peak: 2.3-5.4 miles (RT), strenuous
30. Uncompaghre Peak: 7.8 miles (RT), strenuous-difficult
31. Cataract Lake: 7.6-8.2 miles (RT), moderate-strenuous
32. Grizzly Gulch: 8.0 mile (RT), killer
33. Redcloud and Sunshine Peaks: 9.0 -11.8 miles (RT), killer
34. Devils Lake: 14.0 miles (RT), strenuous
35. Powderhorn Lake: 7.8-9.6 miles (RT), moderate

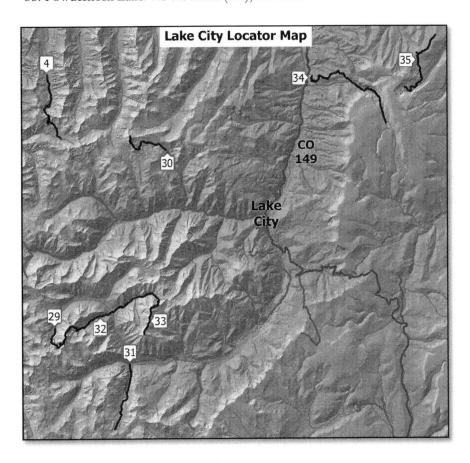

Lake City Locator Map

1. Blue Lakes Pass ★★★★★

Distance: 6.3 - 11.0 miles (RT)

This popular hike visits three scenic lakes in a beautiful glacial basin surrounded by the rugged summits of Mount Sneffels (14,150-ft.), Dallas Peak (13,809-ft.) and Gilpin Peak (13,694-ft.).

Distance: 6.3 miles (RT) to Lower Blue Lakes
8.2 miles (RT) to Upper Blue Lakes
11.0 miles (RT) to Blue Lakes Pass
Elevation: 9,350-ft. at Trailhead
10,940-ft. at Lower Blue Lakes
11,750-ft. at Upper Blue Lakes
13,000-ft. at Blue Lakes Pass
Elevation Gain: 1,590-ft. to Lower Blue Lakes
2,400-ft. to Upper Blue Lakes
3,650-ft. to Blue Lakes Pass

Difficulty: moderate-strenuous
Basecamp: Ouray
Area: Mt. Sneffels Wilderness, Uncompahgre NF
Best Season: July - September
USGS Map(s): Mount Sneffels, Telluride

Why Hike Blue Lakes

Turquoise lakes nestled in dramatic glacial cirques, wildflower-filled alpine meadows ringed by craggy peaks and ridges and a pass with see-forever views makes the Blue Lakes trail a top hike on my "to do list" on every trip to southwest Colorado.

The hike, one of the few in the Mount Sneffels Wilderness, culminates at spectacular Blue Lakes Pass (13,000-ft.) on a steep ridge extending south from Mt. Sneffels (14,150-ft.). Along the way the trail visits three scenic lakes cradled in a beautiful glacial basin set amid rugged ridges and peaks over 13,000-ft.

For an easy day Lower Blue Lake, lying in a pretty cirque dominated by Dallas Peak, makes a worthy destination. From here a short, steep trail leads to the two upper Blue Lakes set beneath the western flanks of Mt. Sneffels in wildflower filled meadows ringed by jagged ridges. Beyond the lakes a demanding trail ascends 1,250-ft. in 1.4 miles to the panoramic viewpoint at the pass.

Trailhead to Lower Blue Lakes

Distance from Trailhead: 6.3 miles (RT)
Elevation: 10,940-ft.
Elevation Gain: 1,590-ft.

Blue Lakes, one of the few trails penetrating the Mt. Sneffels Wilderness, starts at the north end of the Blue Lakes trailhead parking lot (see driving directions below). The trail passes through a gate and soon reaches a "Y" intersection. Our path to Blue Lakes branches right and ascends on moderate grades through a forest of Engelmann Spruce and pines along the right (west) of East Fork Dallas Creek. (The trail to the left leads to Blaine Basin.) Occasional openings in the trees provide tantalizing views of surrounding peaks.

After an hour of climbing meadows provide vistas of the rugged peaks lining the lower basin. Soon after passing an avalanche chute on the east side of Wolcott Mountain the grade abates. You'll know when you are less than 1/3 of a mile from the lower lake when you see a waterfall tumble down a rocky cleft on your left (southeast).

Past the waterfall the trail climbs on moderately steep grades to a junction with a short spur trail to the right (south) leading to the Lower Blue Lake. Acclimated hikers will reach this point in about 1 ½ hours (3.2 miles, 1,500-ft. elevation gain).

Pretty Lower Blue Lake (10,940-ft.), is nestled in a scenic bowl beneath a cirque of jagged peaks dominated by Dallas Peak (13,809-ft.) to the southwest. Mount Sneffels (14,156-ft.) rises to the east. Steep scree slopes spill down the cirque's rugged walls to the southern and western shoreline of the lake. Nice campsites, sheltered by trees, are located on the lake's north shore, with addition sites to the east across the creek.

Lower Blue Lakes to Upper Blue Lakes

Segment Stat: 2.4 miles (one-way) with a 810-ft. elevation gain
Distance - Trailhead to Upper Blue Lake: 8.2 miles (RT)
Elevation Upper Blue Lake: 11,750-ft.
Elevation Gain - Trailhead to Upper Blue Lake: 2,400-ft.

To reach the upper lakes return to the junction and rock-hop across the lake's outlet stream. Follow the trail a short distance and cross to the east side of the East Fork Dallas Creek on a large log. Finding the trail on the other side of the creek can be little confusing due to erosion and use trails leading to campsites.

The way now climbs steeply up the headwall of the lower basin, in route crossing back to the west side of the creek. As you climb trees give way to alpine tundra filled with wildflowers in mid-July. At the top of the cliff the trail reaches a fantastic viewpoint showcasing the lower lake basin.

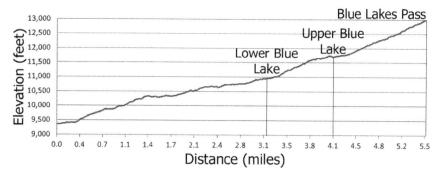

Beyond the viewpoint the climb moderates, passing to the west and above middle Blue Lake to reach Upper Blue Lake after 0.9 miles and a 700-ft. elevation gain. (Total hiking distance: 4.1 miles / 2,350-ft. of elevation gain.)

The upper lake is set amid meadows dotted with wildflowers. A scenic ridge with steep scree slopes tinted bronze, rust and gold extends from Dallas Peak to Gilpin Peak (13,694-ft.), forming the southern wall of the upper basin. The ridge between Gilpin Peak and Mt. Sneffels creates the eastern wall.

While the upper basin is a great destination and the perfect place to relax and take in the scenery, hikers with the time (and good weather) will want to climb to Blue Lakes Pass (13,000-ft), which lies 1,250-ft. above the upper Lake on the ridge extending between Mt. Sneffels and Gilpin Peak.

Upper Lakes to Blue Lakes Pass

Segment Stats: 1.4 miles (one-way) with a 1,250-ft. elevation gain
Distance - Trailhead to Blue Lakes Pass: 11.0 miles (RT)
Elevation Blue Lakes Pass: 13,000-ft.
Elevation Gain - Trailhead to Blue Lakes Pass: 3,650-ft.

To reach the pass follow the well-defined trail around the left (east) side of Upper Blue Lake to a series of long, steep switchbacks. As you ascend fields of wildflowers give way to dirt and talus. Footing is generally good except for a few short, eroded sections.

Take occasional breaks from the climb to admire the wonderful views of the jagged ridges towering above the sapphire Blue Lakes nestled in the upper basin. The top of the pass is reached in 1.4 miles (total distance: 5.5 miles with 3,650-ft. of elevation gain from the trailhead).

The pass offers splendid views to the north of the peaks and ridges defining the Blue Lakes basin. To the south is Yankee Boy Basin dominated by Gilpin Peak (13,694-ft.), Potosi (13,786-ft.) and Teakettle Mountain (13,819-ft.). In the distance a series of peaks and ridges form the northern wall of Yankee Boy Basin.

On the northeast side of the pass a faint trail indicates the start of a Class 3 route climbing Mt. Sneffel's southwest ridge. This route should only be used by parties with prior climbing experience. Most people climb Mt. Sneffels (14,156-ft.) from a well-defined Class 2 route that begins in Yankee Boy basin.

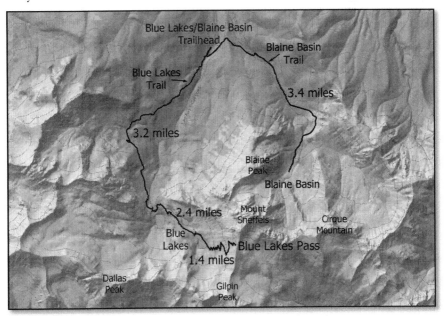

Once you are done soaking in the scenery retrace your steps to the trailhead. Parties with a prepositioned second vehicle can continue over the pass and down to a 4WD road in Yankee Boy Basin (1.4 miles).

Note: This is a popular trail that is best hiked on a weekday if you wish to encounter fewer people on the trail.

Driving Directions

From Ouray: It takes 45-50 minutes to drive the 24 miles from Ouray to the Blue Lakes trailhead. The drive is quite scenic with views dominated by 14,150-ft. Mt. Sneffels and its neighboring peaks and ridges, almost all over 13,000-ft.

From the center of Ouray take Highway 550 heading north for just over 10 miles to Highway 62 in Ridgway. Turn left (west) on Highway 62. Drive 4.8 miles and take a left onto County Road 7, marked Dallas Creek (the road use to be marked East Dallas Creek). It is easy to miss the turn while you are admiring the scenery to the south of the highway. In two miles CR-7 bears right where it meets CR-7A. Continue for a total of 9 miles on CR-7 through a beautiful valley to the parking area at the trailhead. Note: CR-7 turns into Forest Road 851.1 at the forest boundary.

From Telluride: From Telluride the trailhead is a 90 minute/ 44 miles drive. Drive west on West Colorado Avenue to Highway 145. Head west on Hwy 145 12.7 miles to where it dead ends at Highway 62 in Placerville. Take a right (turn east) onto Highway 62 and drive 18.6 miles to County Road 7, marked Dallas Creek (the road use to be marked East Dallas Creek). Turn right onto CR-7. In two miles CR-7 bears right where it meets CR-7A. Continue for a total of 9 miles through a beautiful valley to the parking area at the trailhead. Note: CR-7 turns into Forest Road 851.1 at the forest boundary.

Road Conditions: Passenger cars accessible. CR-7 is a good, graded gravel road up to National Forest boundary. Beyond this point the road maintenance deteriorates and you will need to dodge potholes.

2. Bridge of Heaven ★★★★☆
Distance: 8.0 miles (RT)

This well-engineered trail ascends 3,000-ft. to a knife-edge ridge with spectacular panoramic views.

Distance: 8.0 miles (RT) to Bridge of Heaven
Elevation: 9,300-ft. at Trailhead
 12,300-ft. at Bridge of Heaven
Elevation Gain: 3,000-ft.
Difficulty: strenuous

Basecamp: Ouray, Ridgway
Area: Uncompahgre NF
Best Season: July - September
USGS Map(s): Ouray

Why Hike Bridge of Heaven

Choose a promising day and take a walk to heaven. The aptly named Bridge of Heaven trail leads to a lofty vantage point on a narrow 12,300-ft. ridge with spectacular panoramic views of the Cimarron Range to the northeast, the Sneffels Range to the west and Ironton and Red Mountain Pass to the south.

Getting to heaven takes some effort. The trail ascends 3,000-ft. in 4.0 miles. Thankfully a well-engineered trail makes the climb easier that it sounds. Trailhead access is another issue. Four-wheel drive is required to cross Dexter Creek and negotiate the final 2.2 miles of rough road ascending 700-ft. to the trailhead parking area.

Trailhead to First Viewpoint

Distance from Trailhead: 3.4 miles (RT)
Ending Elevation: 10,385-ft.
Elevation Gain: 1,085-ft.

From the trailhead parking area (see driving directions), walk about 100 yards up the road to the Horsethief trailhead on the right (south side) of the road. The trail immediately starts uphill on a series of well graded switchbacks through a mixed forest of spruce and aspen. After ascending for about 15 minutes sporadic openings in the trees reveal views of Whitehouse Mountain to the west and Ridgway to the north.

At 1.7 miles reach a marked trail junction on a grassy hillside with a sign pointing to a faint trail heading downhill toward Ouray. This is the old Horsethief trail that starts at the northern end of Ouray (the trail was repaired and rerouted in 2004). To the right of the junction is a grassy knoll with wonderful views of Yankee Boy Basin and prominent peaks of the Sneffels range across the valley to the west. To the south you can see the town of Ouray along with the peaks flanking the San Juan Skyway (aka Million Dollar Highway) including Mt. Hayden, Mt. Abrams and, the aptly named, Red Mountain. The viewpoint is a good destination for people

hiking with young children or hikers with limited time looking for a short hike with great views.

First Viewpoint to Bridge of Heaven

Segment Stat: 2.3 miles (one-way) with a 1,915-ft. elevation gain
Distance - Trailhead: 8.0 miles (RT)
Ending Elevation: 12,300-ft.
Elevation Gain - Trailhead to Bridge of Heaven: 3,000-ft.

The trail now travels on mostly open slopes along the south side of a ridge with nice views, passing in and out of isolated pockets of trees. Along the way a few switchbacks ease the ascent.

For a brief period the trail crosses to the north side of the ridge revealing the highly eroded hillsides of the Dexter Creek drainage and the western most peaks of the Cimarron range to the northeast, including distinctive Courthouse Mountain.

At 3.5 miles the trail breaks out of the trees for the last time, crosses a small depression and begins climbing a series of steep switchbacks up a grassy hillside. Expansive and ever improving views of the Cimarron Range, the Sneffels Range and Ironton and the Red Mountain Pass area divert your attention from the stiff climb.

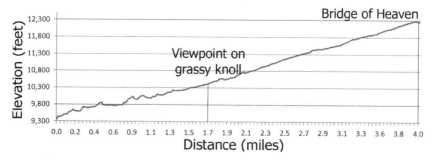

At the top of the hill follow the trail a short distance to a wooden stake marking the Bridge of Heaven, a narrow 20-ft.-long section of the ridge, at 12,300-ft. To get the best views from this amazing vantage point take a short side trip up the dirt knoll on the west side of the Bridge.

From the knoll the magnificent panorama of the Sneffels range and the peaks forming the south and western walls of Yankee Boy Basin fill the skyline to the west. To the south views extends along the San Juan Skyway from Mt. Hayden to the Red Mountains. To the northeast the sculpted peaks of the Cimarron range paint the horizon. To the north is the town of Ridgway. Keep an eye out for bighorn sheep on the rocky ridges below the "Bridge".

Across the "Bridge" to the east the Horsethief trail drops down into a grassy bowl then continues its southeastern course towards Difficulty and American Flats. These destinations are beyond the range of a day hike.

30

After soaking in the scenery retrace your footsteps. The well maintained trail makes it easy to enjoy the views all over again on the descent.

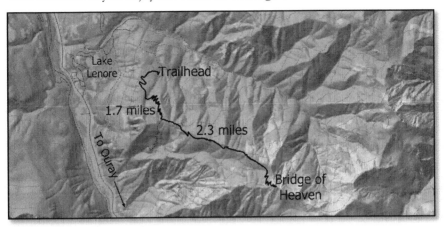

Driving Directions

From Ouray: Drive 2 miles north from the center Ouray on Highway 550 to County Road 14 and turn right. A sign at the turnoff points to the Bachelor-Syracuse Mine tours. Follow County Road 14, a good gravel road, for 1 mile as is winds its way past Lake Lenore and reaches the junction with County Road 14A. Stay on County Road 14 by bearing right at this junction. (CR-14A goes left.) CR-14 continues for 1.5 miles until it reaches a ford with Dexter Creek. (Note: you will first cross Dexter Creek on a bridge at .7 miles. Beyond this point the road becomes a bit rougher). Passenger cars should not ford the creek but instead find parking near the Dexter Creek trailhead, located right before the ford. (Parking before the ford will add 2.2 miles round trip and over 700-ft. of climbing to the hike.)

If you have a 4WD cross the creek and continue up the road for another 1.1 miles to the trailhead parking area on the left. The parking lot is an open area with piles of rock from the Wedge mine. (Note: Please respect the private property on both signs of the road.) The trailhead is located about 100 yards up the road on the right (south).

3. Bear Creek National Recreation Trail

★★★★☆

Distance: 4.4 - 8.0 miles (RT)

A dramatic trail carved into a steep cliff face high above Bear Creek is just one of the highlights of this hike up a beautiful canyon to two scenic mine sites.

Distance: 4.4 miles (RT) to Grizzly Bear Mine
8.0 miles (RT) to Yellow Jacket Mine
Elevation: 8,470-ft. at Trailhead
10,030-ft. at Grizzly Bear Mine
11,130-ft. at Yellow Jacket Mine
Elevation Gain: 1,560-ft. to Grizzly Bear Mine
2,660-ft. to Yellow Jacket Mine
Difficulty: moderate

Basecamp: Ouray, Silverton
Area: Uncompahgre NF
Best Season: July - September
USGS Map(s): Ouray, Ironton, Handies Peak

Why Hike the Bear Creek National Recreation Trail

No matter how many times I hike Bear Creek I still marvel at the effort and ingenuity that went into building this trail. In the 1870's miners discovered large quantities of gold and silver in the Bear Creek basin southeast of Ouray. Accessing the claims proved difficult. A deep gorge, formed by sheer vertical walls rising high above the rugged creek bed, guarded the entrance to the basin. Building a trail in the steep rocky terrain along the creek bottom was not an option. Instead the miners blasted a narrow ledge into the cliff 700-ft. above the gorge.

Today, the Bear Creek National Recreation Trail follows this amazing route up beautiful Bear Creek Canyon. A series of long switchbacks with wonderful views of the Mt. Sneffels range climbs 1,000-ft. up the east side of the Uncompahgre Gorge to reach the traverse of the ledge high above the Bear Creek. Beyond Bear Creek's gorge the trail wanders through forests and alpine meadows beside the creek's tumbling cascades, visiting two scenic abandoned mines along the way.

Trailhead to the Grizzly Bear Mine

Distance from Trailhead: 4.4 miles (RT)
Ending Elevation: 10,030-ft.
Elevation Gain: 1,560-ft.

The Bear Creek National Recreation Trail starts on the west side of Highway 550, 2.5 miles south of Ouray. (See driving directions.) Carefully cross to the west side of the road and then follow the trail as it climbs over a road tunnel to the north of the parking lot. In a short distance reach the trailhead registry and the beginning of a series of long, moderately steep switchback ascending the east side of the Uncompahgre Gorge, a deep mountain canyon formed by the Uncompahgre River and Red Mountain Creek south of Ouray.

The lower sections of the switchbacks climb through a mixed conifer forest passing some impressive old white firs. As the trail gains elevation the trees give way to open slopes. Here the trail ascends through rock slides composed of slate and quartzite. Terrific views open to the Mt. Sneffels range across the valley to the west and the town of Ouray to the north.

Reach the top of the switchbacks in slightly under a mile having gained 1,000-ft. The grade now moderates as the trail enters the Bear Creek drainage, heading east across a talus slope high above Bear Creek. Views to the south extend to Red Mountain pass. A section of the San Juan Skyway (Million Dollar Highway) is visible in the distance.

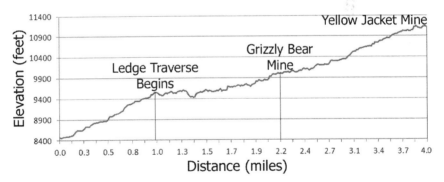

After five minutes the trail levels off following the contours of the canyon's steep walls on a narrow ledge carved into the talus cliff. Footing is generally good except for a few short eroded sections.

One can only image the effort required to build and maintain this route. As you hike along the ledge note how sections of the trail are supported by logs and rubble fill. Across the canyon look for mines dug in the steep canyon walls. The walk along the ledge (0.8 miles) ends where it crosses a rocky drainage.

The trail now ascends moderately on dry slopes with intermittent pockets of trees. About 0.2 miles before the Grizzly Bear Mine the trail enters a nice stand of aspens. Keep an eye out for a metal sided shed on your left. Shortly thereafter mining equipment and a collapsed wood building with a corrugated aluminum roof lie scattered along the side of the trail. This is the Grizzly Bear mine (10,020-ft.), located 2.2 miles and 1,560-ft. from the trailhead.

The mine is a nice destination and a good turn around point for hikers with limited time (and energy). Otherwise, after exploring the area continue the hike to the Yellow Jacket mine, located 1.8 miles ahead.

Grizzly Bear Mine to the Yellow Jacket Mine

Segment Stat: 1.8 miles (one-way) with a 1,100-ft. elevation gain
Distance - Trailhead to Yellow Jacket Mine: 8.0 miles (RT)
Ending Elevation: 11,130-ft.
Elevation Gain - Trailhead to Yellow Jacket Mine: 2,660-ft.

The trail to the Yellow Jacket mine ascends on a moderate grades above the left (north) side of Bear Creek through intermittent forests of mix conifers and aspens. At 2.7 miles (10,200-ft.) rock-hop across a tributary of Bear Creek. Look for a post marking the continuation of the trail on the other side. Shortly after crossing the stream the path traverses a pretty wildflower-filled meadow with views of peaks to the north and east.

The trail now continues its moderate ascent, aided by occasional switchbacks, through meadows and trees. Reach the Yellow Jacket mine (11,130) at 4.0 miles having gained over 2,660-ft. The site, flanked by steep grassy meadows and talus slopes, is littered with mine debris and includes a photogenic wood building. To the west distant views of the Mt. Sneffels range fill the skyline.

Slightly beyond the mine site a signposts points the way to the Horsethief trail, which ultimately leads to the Bridge of Heaven and Engineer Pass. Both destinations are too far for a day hike.

To complete your hike, return the way you came.

Driving Directions

From Ouray: Take Highway 550 (aka the Million Dollar Highway) 2.5 miles south of Ouray. The trailhead parking lot is on the east side (left) of the road immediately after the road passed through a small tunnel. The trailhead is on west side (right) of the road.

4. Wetterhorn Basin ★★★★★
Distance: 5.8 - 9.0 miles (RT)

This trail wanders through wildflower-filled meadows and then climbs a gorgeous alpine basin to West Fork Pass. From the pass the trail drops into scenic Wetterhorn Basin with great views of Wetterhorn Peak (14,015-ft.).

Distance: 5.8 miles (RT) to West Fork Pass
9.0 miles (RT) to Wetterhorn Basin
Elevation: 10,760-ft. at the Trailhead
12,517-ft. at West Fork Pass
11,850-ft. at Wetterhorn Basin
Elevation Gain: 1,757-ft. to West Fork Pass
-667-ft. to Wetterhorn Basin
Difficulty: moderate

Basecamp: Ouray, Ridgway
Area: Uncompahgre Wilderness, Uncompahgre NF
Best Season: July - September
USGS Map(s): Courthouse Mountain, Wetterhorn Peak

Why Hike Wetterhorn Basin

Heading south on Highway 550 near Ridgway a panorama of alluring summits and jagged ridges of the Uncompahgre Wilderness fill the eastern skyline, enticing hikers to explore. Several trails penetrate this wilderness from the north traveling up pretty valleys to scenic passes with dramatic mountain views.

In my opinion the Wetterhorn Basin trail is the finest hike entering the area from the north. The trail gently ascends the beautiful West Fork Cimarron River valley, wandering through scenic meadows beneath Fortress (13-241-ft.), Redcliff (13,642-ft.) and Coxcomb (13,654-ft.) peaks to the head of the valley, where it climbs a gorgeous alpine basin to West Fork Pass (12,517-ft.).

Just beyond the pass viewpoints showcase stunning Wetterhorn Peak (14,015-ft.) and the emerald green meadows of Wetterhorn Basin. A great lunch spot on the ridge just below the pass offers panoramic views of the basin, the peaks towering above Cow Creek drainage to the southwest and the Sneffels range to the west. Alternatively hike into the basin to the base of Wetterhorn Peak for a more intimate view.

Trailhead to West Fork Pass

Distance from Trailhead: 5.8 miles (RT)
Ending Elevation: 12,517-ft.
Elevation Gain: 1,757-ft.

Few trails boast the stunning view seen from the start of the Wetterhorn Basin hike. From the 4WD trailhead (see driving directions below) Redcliff and Coxcomb Peaks dominate the view at the head of the valley, rising above flower-filled meadows and spruce-fir forests. Our destination is the pass to the west of Coxcomb.

The well-defined trail stays to the left (east) of the West Fork of the Cimarron river, ascending on easy gradient through open meadows before entering the forest at 0.7 miles. Openings in the trees provide intermittent views of the surrounding ridges defining the valley. Along the way the trail crosses side steams and avalanche chutes, emerging at a beautiful alpine basin at the head of the valley in just over 1.6 miles (11,370-ft.).

Cross a side stream and head west across the basin to a series of switchbacks ascending toward the pass through grassy meadows sprinkled with columbines, Indian paintbrush and buttercups. As you climb the trail crosses to the west side of the West Fork, now just a pretty stream cascading down the hillside.

Across the valley Precipice, Fortress, Redcliff and Coxcomb peaks punctuate the ridge forming the valley's eastern wall. To the north views open to distinctive Courthouse Mountain and Chimney Rock.

The grade abates briefly then ascends a steep slope of loose talus and boulders. Beyond the talus the trail climbs a grassy knoll dotted with wildflowers, reaching the West Fork Pass (12,517-ft.) in 2.9-miles after gaining 1,757-ft.

Coxcomb Peak rises to the east of the pass. To the south enjoy great views of the peaks and ridges towering above the Wetterhorn and Cow Creek drainages – but not of Wetterhorn Peak.

Pass to Wetterhorn Lookout

Segment Stat: 0.5 miles (one-way) with a net -261-ft. elevation loss
Distance - Trailhead to Lookout: 6.8 miles (RT)
Ending Elevation: 12,256-ft.
Elevation Gain - Trailhead to Lookout: +1,857-ft./-261-ft.

To see Wetterhorn Peak climb a short distance up the ridge to the west or follow the obvious use trail contouring to the west just below the south side of the pass. The idea is to get above or to the right (west) of a ridge extending from Coxcomb Peak that is blocking the view of Wetterhorn Peak.

For more expansive views I recommend hiking down the south side of the pass for about 0.3 miles (losing about 330-ft.) and then heading right (west) across a rocky meadow to an obvious use trail climbing steeply about 100-ft. up a ridge jutting into the basin. From the end of the ridge enjoy stunning views of Wetterhorn Peak towering above the emerald green basin and bird's eye views into Cow Creek and Wetterhorn creek drainages to the south. The Mt. Sneffels range graces the skyline to the west.

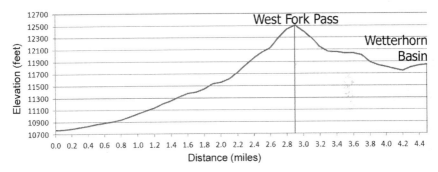

Pass to Wetterhorn Basin

Segment Stat: 1.6 miles (one-way) with a +100-ft./-750-ft. elevation gain/loss
Distance - Trailhead to Wetterhorn Basin: 9.0 miles (RT)
Ending Elevation: 11,850-ft.
Elevation Gain - Trailhead to the Basin: 1,857-ft. / -750-ft.

For a more intimate view of Wetterhorn Peak follow the trail down the south side of the pass into the basin. The trail drops over 750-ft. then climbs about 100-ft. to Wetterhorn Creek in 1.6 miles. (Total round trip from the trailhead to the creek is 9-miles.) From this vantage point pyramid-shaped Wetterhorn Peak pierces the skyline to the east while distinctive Coxcomb Peak looms to the north.

Driving Directions

From Ouray: Head north from Ouray on US Highway 550 for just under 12 miles and turn right (east) onto Owl Creek Road (CR10 - Ouray County 10). The turn is 1.8 miles past the turnoff to Ridgway (Highway 62). Follow the signs to Owl Creek Pass (14.9 miles). Along the way CR 10 turns into CR 8 and then FR 858 after crossing into the Uncompahgre National Forest. As you drive toward the pass enjoy views of Courthouse Mountain and Chimney Rock. Continue over the pass for 0.3 miles to FR 860 (West Fork Road). Turn right and follow FR 860 for 3.3 miles to the trailhead with ample parking. The last 1.5 miles of the road are very rocky and requires a high clearance or 4WD.

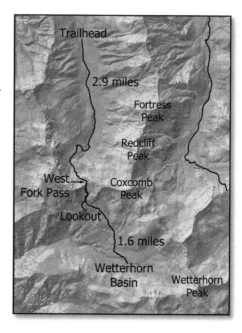

5. Blaine Basin ★★★★★
Distance: 6.8 miles (RT)

This is a good hike for people looking for solitude and dramatic, up-close views of the north face of Mt. Sneffels (14,150-ft.). Don't let the crowded parking lot deter you. Most hikers are headed for the Blue Lakes basin. You will have the Blaine Basin trail mostly to yourself.

Distance: 6.8 - 8.2 miles (RT) to Blaine Basin
Elevation: 9,350-ft. at Trailhead 11,200-ft. at Blaine Basin
Elevation Gain: 1,850-ft. to Blaine Basin
Difficulty: moderate

Basecamp: Ouray, Ridgway
Area: Mt. Sneffels Wilderness, Uncompahgre NF
Best Season: July - September
USGS Map(s): Ouray
See Page 27 for Map

Why Hike Blaine Basin

Looking for a little solitude? Then take a hike to Blaine Basin.

This lightly used trail does not require a lot of effort and culminates in a scenic wildflower-filled basin with great views of Mt. Sneffels (14,156-ft.), Kismet (13,694-ft.) and Cirque Mountain (13,868-ft.). Along the way the trail wanders through forests, passes a pretty waterfall and crosses Wilson Creek three times.

Looking for more of a challenge? Then climb the steep, off-trail route to a high bench between Mt. Sneffels and Blaine Peak for close-up views of Sneffels and a bird's-eye view of the basin.

Be forewarned, the trailhead parking area is often overflowing down the access road. Don't let the crowded parking lot deter you. Most hikers are headed for the Blue Lakes trail. You will likely have the Blaine Basin trail mostly to yourself.

Trailhead to Blaine Basin

Distance from Trailhead: 6.8 miles (RT)
Ending/Highest Elevation: 11,200-ft.
Elevation Gain: 1,850-ft.

This hike shares the trailhead parking area with the Blue Lakes trail (see driving directions). Walk through the gate at the northern end of the parking lot and in a short distance reach a "Y" intersection. Turn left at the sign pointing to Blaine Basin (about 300-ft. from the gate.) The trail to the right goes to Blue Lakes.

In a few hundred yards the trail, an old logging road, crosses the East Fork Dallas Creek on a wood bridge. Follow the road as is ascends on moderate grades through spruce-fir forest, ignoring two minor roads branching to the right.

At 0.6 miles the trail crosses a low ridge and enters the Wilson Creek drainage. The grade abates as the path traverses aspen groves and meadows to meet Wilson Creek at 0.6 miles. Backtrack a brief distance from the crossing to find a rock cairn marking a trail heading right and leading to a

makeshift bridge, constructed of logs, crossing the creek. Across the creek join a road switchbacking up to the right.

Beyond the crossing reach a trail junction and turn right (east/southeast) on the trail signed for Blaine Basin. The trail to the left is the East Dallas trail that descends to the East Dallas Road.

For the next 0.8 miles the trail meanders through forest with intermittent meadows, paralleling the creek and crossing its two more times at 1.6 miles and 2.0 miles. Just after the third crossing look for a pretty waterfall cascading down the cliff face to the right (southwest) of the trail.

At 2.2 miles a sign marks a junction where the trail curves to the left (east). Ignore the unmarked trail to the right that leads to the base of the falls. Past the sign the path starts ascending on moderately-steep grades, reaching a signed junction with the Dallas Trail, branching left, at 2.3 miles. Continue straight ahead on the Blaine Basin trail.

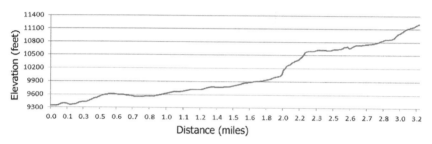

The rocky trail now climbs a steep slope through trees. Near the top of the slope the trail ascends through a small meadow and then turns right (south) toward the creek. Follow the trail as it climbs on moderate grades through trees and emerges in a beautiful meadow near Wilson Creek at 3.0 miles. This is lower Blaine Basin.

The meadow provides the first views of the north face of Mt. Sneffels (14,150-ft.), rising to the southwest. For even better views follow the trail as it crosses the creeks and climbs gently through meadows filled with wildflowers in season. Soon the trail starts climbing steep switchbacks up a hillside scattered with small trees, passing a sign for Blaine Basin at 3.2 miles. The smaller trees indicate the path of avalanches thundering down Sneffel's north face.

After a short climb reach the upper basin (11,120-ft.) at 3.4 miles. The trail ends at a lovely lookout. In season, the fields of the upper basin are filled with a spectacular display of wildflowers. Mt. Sneffels towers above the scenic basin with Kismet (13,694-ft.) and Cirque Mountain (13,680-ft.) rising to east of Sneffels. To the right (west) is Blaine Peak (12,910-ft.). Glacial moraines clearly illustrate the paths of ancient glaciers that once filled the basin.

A faint use trail is visible climbing the slope to a high bench between Mt. Sneffels and Blaine Peak. If time, energy and weather permit, the off-trail route to the bench offers up close views of Sneffels and bird's-eye views of the basin.

Route to the Bench

Segment Stat: 0.7 mile (one-way) with 880-ft. elevation loss
Distance from Trailhead: 8.2 miles (RT)
Ending/Highest Elevation: 12,080-ft.
Elevation Gain: 2,730-ft.

To reach the bench, walk a short distance up the valley and cross to the right (west) side of a rocky gully. On the other side of the gully continue ascending the valley until you find a good place to climb the grassy slopes to the use trail seen from the lookout. Follow the use trail as it switchbacks up the grassy slope to the south of Blaine Peak.

The trail fades as it reaches a gully carrying meltwater from the north slopes of Mt. Sneffels. Under good conditions you can cross the gully and find a trail on the other side that continues to the Blaine Mine. On my recent trip to the basin ice and loose rock filled the gully, preventing a safe crossing. In this case I simply climbed the grassy slopes to the right (northwest) of the gully until I reached the high bench overlooking Blaine Basin. From the bench enjoy lovely, up-close views of Mt Sneffel's north face and Cirque Mountain to the southeast. This side trip gains almost 900 feet in just 0.7 miles, adding 1.4 miles to the round trip hiking distance.

Many people will be happy simply exploring the scenic upper basin and taking pictures of the wildflowers. When you are done enjoying the basin retrace your steps to the trailhead parking area.

Driving Directions

From Ouray: It takes 45-50 minutes to drive the 24 miles from Ouray to the Blaine Basin trailhead (shared with the Blue Lakes trail). The drive is quite scenic with views dominated by 14,150-ft. Mt. Sneffels and its neighboring peaks and ridges, almost all over 13,000-ft.

From the center of Ouray take Highway 550 heading north for just over 10 miles to Highway 62 in Ridgway. Turn left (west) on Highway 62. Drive 4.8 miles and take a left onto County Road 7, marked Dallas Creek (older signs called the road East Dallas Creek). It is easy to miss the turn while you are admiring the scenery to the south of the highway. In two miles CR-7 bears right where it meets CR-7A. Continue for a total of 9 miles on CR-7 through a beautiful valley to the parking area at the trailhead. Note: CR-7 turns into Forest Road 851.1 at the forest boundary.

From Telluride: From Telluride the trailhead is a 90 minute/ 44 miles drive. Drive west on West Colorado Avenue to Highway 145. Head west on Hwy 145 12.7 miles to where it dead ends at Highway 62 in Placerville. Take a right (turn east) onto Highway 62 and drive 18.6 miles to County Road 7, marked Dallas Creek (older signs called the road East Dallas Creek). Turn right onto CR-7. In two miles CR-7 bears right where it meets CR-7A. Continue for a total of 9 miles through a beautiful valley to the parking area at the trailhead. Note: CR-7 turns into Forest Road 851.1 at the forest boundary.

Road Conditions: Passenger car accessible. CR-7 is a good, graded gravel road up to National Forest boundary. Beyond this point the road maintenance deteriorates and you will need to dodge potholes.

6. Upper Cascade Falls ★★★★★
Distance: 4.4 - 5.9 miles (RT)

This great half day hike climbing high above the eastern side of Ouray features panoramic views of the Uncompahgre Valley, Cascade Falls and the Amphitheater.

Distance: 4.4 miles (RT) to Upper Cascade Falls
5.9 miles (loop) with return via the Portland Trail
Elevation: 8,500-ft. at Trailhead
10,030-ft. at Upper Cascade Falls
Elevation Gain: 1,530-ft. to Upper Cascade Falls
Difficulty: moderate-strenuous

Basecamp: Ouray
Area: Uncompahgre NF
Best Season: July - September
USGS Map(s): Ouray

Why Hike Upper Cascade Falls Trail

Scenic views of the amphitheater rock formation, Upper Cascade Falls and Ouray along with a good workout are the rewards of this half day hike, located just a mile south of Ouray. Links to the Portland and the Lower Cascade Falls trails create interesting options to extend the trip. The length of the hike, its close proximity to town and good views make it a nice option if the weather is expected to turn for the worse later in the day.

Trailhead to Upper Cascade Falls

Distance from Trailhead: 4.4 miles (RT)
Elevation Upper Cascade Falls: 10,030-ft.
Elevation Gain: 1,530-ft.

The trail to Upper Cascade Falls starts at the southeast end of a small parking area at the top of the Amphitheater Campground (see driving directions below). Follow the trail for 0.2 miles as it contours along the hillside to a trail junction. At the junction turn left on the Upper Cascade Falls trail toward the Chief Ouray Mine. The trail to the right, the Portland Trail, can be used as a return leg of an extended loop hike.

Climb through scrub oaks and mixed conifers to a second junction, located just over 0.5 miles from the trailhead. Stay on the Upper Cascade trail heading toward the Chief Ouray Mine. The trail to the left heads downhill toward the campground and Lower Cascade falls. This section of the trail enjoys nice views to the west and southwest toward Potosi Peak and Hayden Mountain.

Beyond the junction the grade steepens. Openings in the foliage offer tantalizing views of the sculpted walls of the amphitheater circling the eastern end of the basin. After hiking 0.3 miles reach a second junction with the Portland trail, which branches right. We bear left, following the signs toward Chief Ouray Mine.

The trail now ascends a dry hillside on steep switchbacks, gaining over 1,100-ft in just under a mile. As you climb enjoy wonderful views of the amphitheater. Hayden Mountain and the peaks and ridges around Potosi Peak dominate the scene to the west and southwest.

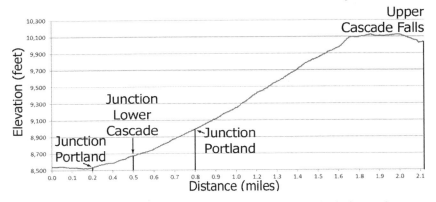

At the top of the switchback the path traverses a rocky ledge and crosses a ridge. Vantage points along the path offer views of Twin Peaks and the Sneffels range to the west and the town of Ouray 2,300-ft below.

After crossing the ridge the trail curves northeast (right) and descends through trees for 0.3 miles to cross the creek at Upper Cascade Falls. Opening in the trees provide views of the Chief Ouray bunkhouse building across the drainage. (The bunkhouse is a light blue metal building.)

43

There are actually two waterfalls, one above the trail and one below. The waterfall below the trail can be heard buy not seen.

After enjoy the secluded area around the falls you can either return the way you came or walk another 0.2 miles to the mine buildings. This section of the trail is not recommended for people with a fear of heights.

Return via the Portland Trail

Distance from Trailhead: 5.9 mile (loop)
Ending Elevation: 8,500-ft. at the trailhead
Elevation Gain/Loss: -1,530-ft.

Return the way you came or extend the hike by turning left (east) onto the Portland trail. The junction is located at the base of the switchbacks. Returning via the well signed Portland trail adds 1.5 miles to the hike and is highly recommended. The trail features wonderful views of the amphitheater and the peaks rising to the south and west of Ouray. See the Portland trail description for more information.

Driving Directions

From Ouray: Drive south from Ouray on Highway 550 for just over a mile to the Amphitheater Campground and turn left onto the campground access road. The turnoff is past the second switchback leaving town. Follow the paved road into the campground for 1.25 miles, keeping left at all intersections. The trailhead, marked for the Upper Cascade trail, is located at the top of the campground. A good hand-drawn map on a signpost at the trailhead shows the interconnecting trail system that includes the Portland Trail, the Upper and Lower Cascade Falls trails and the Portland Mine Road.

44

7. Portland Trail ★★★☆☆

Distance: 3.5 - 4.2 miles (RT)

This short, easy loop hike explores the basin below a huge amphitheater of eroded cliffs rising above the eastern side of Ouray and features scenic viewpoints to appreciate the formation along with the peaks rising to the south and west of town.

Distance: 3.5 miles (loop) with return via Upper Cascade Trail or 4.2 miles (RT)
Elevation: 8,500-ft. at Trailhead 9,250-ft. at high point on the Portland Trail
Elevation Gain: 750-ft. to high point on the Portland Trail
Difficulty: easy

Basecamp: Ouray
Area: Uncompahgre NF
Best Season: July - September
USGS Map(s): Ouray
See Page 44 for Map

Why Hike the Portland Trail

The Amphitheater, a huge sculpted gray cliff face formed from highly eroded volcanic rock, rises above a large bowl-shaped valley on the eastern side of Ouray. A short, easy loop hike, combining the Portland Trail with a portion of the Upper Cascade Falls trail, explores the basin below the amphitheatre and features scenic viewpoints to appreciate the formation along with the peaks rising to the south and west of Ouray. The walk is a good option for those with limited time or on a day when the weather precludes hiking at higher elevations.

The Portland Trail can be extended into a longer hike when combined with the Upper Cascade Falls trail. See the description of the Upper Cascade Falls trail for more information.

Portland Trail Out and Back

Distance: 4.2 miles (RT)
Ending/Highest Elevation: 9,250-ft.
Elevation Gain: 750-ft.

There are several different access points to get on the Portland trail. I prefer starting at the Upper Cascade Falls trailhead, located at the top of the Amphitheater Campground (see driving directions).

Follow the trail, which starts at the southeast end of the small trailhead parking area, for 0.2 miles as it contours along the hillside to a trail junction. Turn right at the junction on the Portland trail. The trail to the left, the Upper Cascade Falls trail, will be used as a return leg of the loop hike.

From the junction the trails descends to cross a normally dry drainage, climbs out the other side and starts ascending the basin on a series of gentle switchbacks. About a half a mile beyond the trailhead you will come to second trail junction. Continue heading northeast in the direction of the scenic overlook indicated on the sign. [The Portland trailhead, pointing to the southwest on the sign, leads to a second trailhead on the Portland Mine Road. This is a good starting point if the campground is closed (see driving directions below)].

Beyond the junction the trail climbs through mixed conifers and small sections of scrub oak. Openings in the foliage feature nice views to the west and southwest toward Hayden Mountain and the peaks and ridges around Potosi Peak. About 1.7-miles from the campground trailhead an opening provides views across the drainage to a mining operation at the southern end of the Amphitheater.

At the 2.0 mile mark a sign points to a scenic overlook with great views of the amphitheatre towering above the basin and Hayden Mountain. Shortly after the overlook (0.1-mile) reach a three-way trail junction.

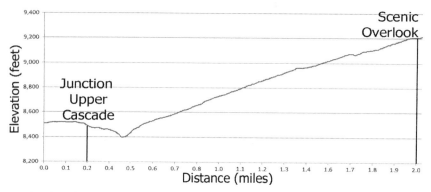

At the three way intersection you have several options. I recommend going left in the direction of the Amphitheater Campground to complete the loop hike. The trail drops down to cross a normally dry drainage and then ascends to meet the Upper Cascade Falls trail in 0.6 miles. Go left at the Cascade Falls trail junction toward the Amphitheater Campground. (The trail to the right climbs 1,100-ft in just under a mile on its way to Upper Cascade Falls and the Chief Ouray Mine.) At the next two junctions follow the signs back to the Campground and the trailhead parking area. See the Upper Cascade description for more information.

Another option is to take a side trip to the Portland Mine. To visit the mine head right at the three way junction, following the trail to the mine. The route drops about 150-ft to cross Portland Creek and then climbs to join the Portland Road in 0.5 miles. Follow the road east to the mine.

Finally, you can simply turn around at the three-way junction and return the way you came. The out-and-back hike is 4.2 miles (RT) from the campground or 3.8 miles (RT) from the trailhead on the Portland Road (see driving directions).

Driving Directions

From Ouray: Drive south from Ouray on Highway 550 for just over a mile to the Amphitheatre Campground and turn left onto the campground access road. The turnoff is past the second switchback leaving town. Follow the paved road into the campground for 1.25 miles, keeping left at all intersections. The trailhead, marked for the Upper Cascade trail, is located at the top of the campground. A good hand-drawn map on a signpost at the trailhead shows the interconnecting trail system that includes the Portland Trail, the Upper and Lower Cascade Falls trails and the Portland Mine Road..

If the access gate to the campground is closed you can reach the Portland trail by walking up the campground road or use two alternative access points. The first access point is reached using the Baby Bathtubs trail. After turning left onto the campground road look for a parking area on your left, right before a bridge. The Baby Bathtubs trail starts on the right side of the road just past the bridge. Follow this trail for just over 0.3 miles to where it meets the Portland trail.

The second access is on the Portland Road. From the Amphitheater Campground road junction at U.S. 550 turn into the campground, follow the road for about 100 yards and turn right on the Portland Road, an unmarked dirt road. Follow the Portland Road for about 0.25 miles to the Portland Trailhead (the first road to the left). This section of the Portland trail crosses a small foot bridge over Portland Creek and ties into the loop trail system in a few hundred yards.

8. Alpine Mine Overlook ★★★★☆

Distance: 5.6 miles (RT)

Hikers completing the stiff climb to an overlook 3,000-ft. above Ouray are rewarded with panoramic views of Ouray, the amphitheatre and the sea of peaks and ridges rising to the east of town.

Distance: 5.6 miles (RT) to Alpine Mine Overlook
Elevation: 8,750-ft. at Trailhead
 10,930-ft. at Alpine Mine Overlook
Elevation Gain: 2,180-ft. to Alpine Mine Overlook
Difficulty: moderate-strenuous

Basecamp: Ouray
Area: Uncompahgre NF
Best Season: July - September
USGS Map(s): Ouray, Ironton

Why Hike to the Alpine Mine Overlook

Perched 3,130-ft above Ouray, the Alpine Mine Overlook features 180-degree panoramic views of the Ouray area and the wall of cliffs and mountains rising to the east. Hayden Mountain and the peaks looming above the Million Dollar Highway dominate the scene to the south and southeast.

The half-day hike to the overlook is a good workout and a great way to acclimate, climbing over 2,000-ft in just under 3-miles. Along the way hikers are treated to close-up views of Hayden Mountain and the jagged cliff face defining the western wall of the Weehawken Valley.

Be aware that you will not be alone on the popular hike, located just 3-miles to the west of Ouray.

Trailhead to Junction with the Alpine Mine Trail

Distance from Trailhead: 1.5 miles (one-way)
Ending Elevation: 9,980-ft.
Elevation Gain: 1,230-ft.

The trail to the Alpine Mine Overlook starts at the Weehawken trailhead (see driving direction). Follow the trail as it ascends moderate to moderately steep switchbacks through a forest of aspen and mixed conifers up the hillside to the north of Weehawken Creek. As you climb the trees give way to open meadows interspersed with aspen groves. The meadows provide nice views of Hayden Mountain across Canyon Creek valley. After about a mile of hiking the trees thicken and restrict the views.

Reach a junction with the Alpine Mine trail at 1.5 miles. Before turning right on the Alpine Mine trail continue a few feet up to the Weehawken trail to a clearing that provides nice views of the cliff face forming the western wall of the Weehawken drainage.

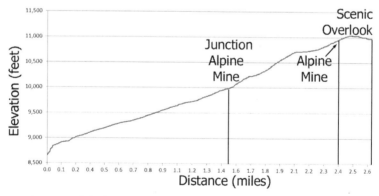

Junction to Alpine Mine Overlook

Segment Stat: 1.3 miles (one-way) with a 950-ft. elevation gain
Distance - Trailhead to Overlook: 5.6 miles (RT)
Maximum Elevation: 10,950-ft.
Elevation Gain - Trailhead to Overlook: 2,180-ft.

Beyond the junction the trail continues its ascent on a series of short, steep switchbacks that gain over 700-ft in 0.7-miles. Toward the top of the

48

switchbacks the trail traverses a steep meadow. At the top of the meadow views open to the sculpted hillside above the trail.

The grade abates a bit as the trail traverses the scree covered slopes of a steep drainage on a narrow footpath with some exposure. Reach the head of the drainage and the site of the Alpine Mine at 2.4 miles. Here you will see mining equipment and remnants of tracks for ore cars. Mine buildings are located in the trees above the trail.

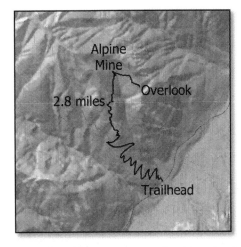

Beyond the mine the path ascends 180-ft in 0.2 miles to reach the top of a ridge and the high point of the trail at 10,950-ft. Follow the trail along the top of the dry ridge interspersed with mixed conifers to the first lookout point featuring great views to the southwest of Potosi Peak and the sculpted cliff face towering above Weehawken Creek. Hayden Mountain and the peaks and ridges along the Million Dollar Highway rise to the southeast.

Continue along the ridge to a sign marking the path through the trees to the Alpine Mine Overlook. The overlook features 180-degree panoramic views. Ouray lies deep in the valley below with a wall of cliffs and mountains rising to the east. The Amphitheater rock formation towers above the southeast end of town. Twin Mountains dominates the view to the north while the peaks along the Million Dollar Highway and Hayden Mountain fill the skyline to the south.

The overlook is quite exposed with sheer drop-offs. Care should be taken while ogling the scenery. This is not a good place for small children.

After admiring the view return the way you came.

Driving Directions

From Ouray: Drive south on US Highway 550 for approximately 0.25 miles. Turn right onto Colorado State Highway 361 (Camp Bird Road) and continue for another 2.7 miles to the Weehawken Trailhead on the right side of the road.

9. Ice Lake Trail ★★★★★
Distance: 7.0 - 8.2 miles (RT)

This wonderful hike visits two gorgeous lake basins, traverses wildflower-filled meadows and passes numerous waterfalls along the way. Dramatic peaks punctuate the ridge forming the backdrop for upper Ice Lake, nestled in an alpine wonderland. Opportunities for exploration include side trips to Island and Fuller lakes.

Distance: 7.0 miles (RT) to Ice Lake
8.2 miles (RT) to Island Lake
Elevation: 9,840-ft. - Trailhead
12,270-ft. - Ice Lake
12,392-ft. - Island Lake
Elevation Gain: 2,430-ft. from trailhead to Ice Lake
2,552-ft. from trailhead to Island Lake
Difficulty: moderate-strenuous

Basecamp: Silverton, Ouray
Area: Part of the San Miguel Roadless Area, San Juan NF
Best Season: July - September
USGS Map(s): Ophir

Why Hike Ice Lakes

The Silverton area boasts a number of great day hikes but none can compete with the sheer scenic beauty of Ice Lake.

The trail wastes no time gaining elevation, climbing 1,600-ft. in 2-miles through forests and wildflower-filled meadows to the beautiful Lower Ice Lakes basin. Upon reaching the lower basin great views open to Fuller, Vermillion Peak, Golden Horn and Pilot Knob rising above the ridge at the head of the basin.

As you wander up the lower basin waterfalls emanating from unseen alpine lakes and snowfields tumble down clefts in the rocky hillside watering a breathtaking array of wildflowers. A sea of columbine, larkspur, aspen daisies, chiming bells and cow parsnips blankets both sides of the trail.

But the best is yet to come. A steep climb to the upper basin leads to the turquoise blue waters of Ice Lake nestled in a magnificent cirque of sculpted ridges and peaks soaring well above 13,000-ft. The alpine tundra wonderland around the lake invites exploration, with routes heading toward Island Lake, Fuller Lake and beyond.

Trailhead to Lower Ice Lake Basin

Distance from Trailhead: 2.25 miles (one-way), 4.5 miles (RT)
Elevation Lower Ice Lake Basin: 11,510-ft.
Elevation Gain: 1,670-ft.

The head of the South Mineral Valley is the starting point for Ice Lake, one of the premier hikes in the San Juan Mountains. The signed trail departs from the west end of the trailhead parking lot, located across from the South Mineral Campground (see driving directions below).

The trail crosses a meadow and starts climbing through trees on moderately steep switchbacks. At 0.4 miles the path crosses Clear Creek and ascends the slope to the west of the creek on well graded switchbacks with intermittent views of Twin Sisters rising across the valley to the south.

After 30 minutes a detour to the right (east) leads to a scenic waterfall tumbling down the rocky hillside. An old wooden bridge crosses the creek beneath the falls. Do not cross the bridge instead return to the main trail.

Beyond the waterfall the trail heads west, climbing steeply up a grassy slope filled with wildflowers. Keep a lookout for the ruins of an abandoned mining building and equipment on your left. The grade abates as the trail crosses a meadow and then enters the trees. The trail now climbs steep switchbacks up a headwall to the Lower Ice Lake basin.

After gaining 1,600-ft. in 2 miles the trail crests the ridge into the beautiful Lower Ice Lake basin. Rock outcroppings provide a nice place to rest and enjoy the view of Fuller (13,761-ft.), Vermillion Peak (13,894-ft.), Golden Horn (13,780-ft.) and Pilot Knob (13,738-ft.) rising above the ridge at the head of the lower basin.

Lower Ice Lake to Ice Lake

Segment Stat: 1.25 miles (one-way) from Lower to Upper Ice Lakes with **760-ft. elevation gain**
Distance - Trailhead to Ice Lake: 7.0 miles (RT)
Elevation at Ice Lake: 12,270-ft.
Elevation Gain - Trailhead to Ice Lake: 2,430-ft.

The trail now traverses lovely meadows on gentle grades, passing Lower Ice Lake nestled in trees to the left (south). Waterfalls, emanating from unseen alpine lakes and snowfields tumble down clefts in the rocky hillside to the north of the trail. During late July to early August the well-watered meadows around the falls host spectacular wildflower displays. Masses of columbines, larkspur, aspen daisies, chiming bells and cow parsnips blanket both sides of the trail.

At the head of the lower basin the trail curves left (south) and starts a steep ascent up the basin's headwall. Ahead you will see a waterfall on the outlet stream for Fuller Lake cascading down a rocky crevasse. Just before reaching the waterfall the trail swings to the left (north) for the final stiff climb to the upper basin. Reach the top of the headwall in 0.6 miles after gaining 700-ft. in elevation.

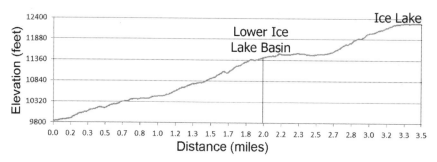

The grade now abates as the trail traverse alpine tundra for the final quarter mile to Ice Lake (12,270-ft.). As you walk toward the lake note the faint trail climbing the grassy slope on your right (north). This trail leads to Island Lake.

Turquoise blue Ice Lake sits in a magnificent cirque amid subalpine tundra dotted with wildflowers. U.S. Grant Peak (13,767-ft.) rises to the north. In a clockwise direction the sculpted peaks and ridges of Fuller Peak (13,761-ft.), Vermillion Peak (13,894-ft.), Golden Horn (13,780-ft.) and Pilot Knob (13,738-ft.) form the southwestern wall of the upper lake basin.

Return to the trailhead by reversing your route or, if you have time, take a side trip to Island or Fuller Lakes. (See descriptions below.)

Optional Side Trip: Ice Lake to Island Lake

Segment Stats: 0.7 miles (one-way) from Ice Lake to Island Lake with a 130-ft. elevation gain
Distance from Trailhead to Island Lake: 8.4 miles (RT)
Elevation Island Lake: 12,392-ft.
Elevation Gain from Trailhead: 2,552-ft.

A side trip to Island Lake (12,392-ft.) is well worth the effort. To reach the lake cross Ice Lake's outlet stream (to find the best place to cross wander downstream a bit) and follow the faint trail climbing the grassy slope to the northeast. The trail is initially hard to see but becomes better defined further up the slope. As you climb, enjoy stunning views of the upper and lower Ice Lake basins.

The trail crosses the base of a tailings pile and then ascends above a rocky outcrop before swinging left (north). The grade now abates as the trail traverses a hillside above the lake. The aquamarine lake is nestled in an intimate cirque at the base of U.S. Grant Peak. If you look carefully, you will see a faint trail climbing the talus ridge to the north of the lake. This route leads to the Ophir Valley. Total distance to Island Lake from Ice Lake is just over 0.7 miles with a 130-ft elevation gain.

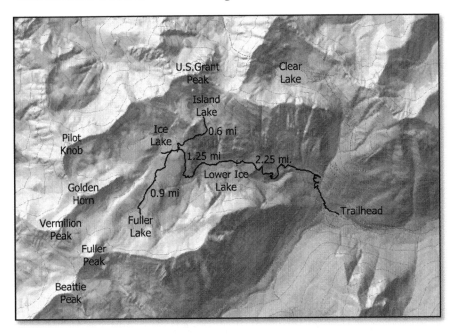

Optional Side Trip: Island Lake to Fuller Lake

Segment Stats: 0.9 miles (one-way) from Ice Lake to Fuller Lake with a 335-ft. elevation gain.
Distance from Trailhead to Fuller Lake: 8.9 miles (RT)
Elevation Fuller Lake: 12,605-ft.
Elevation Gain from Trailhead: 2,765-ft.

The gentle rolling hillsides beyond Ice Lake invite exploration. One popular side trip is the short hike to Fuller Lake. To reach Fuller Lake (12,605-ft.) head up the hill to the south/southwest of Ice Lake to a pond. (There is now a use trail, which fades in places, to help keep you on track.) Go around the left (east) side of the pond and then climb up the open hillside to the south/southwest of the pond. At the top of the hill is a broad shelf. The way to Fuller Lake should now be obvious. Cross a small creek and then travel along the west side of the creek to Fuller Lake. The lake is 0.9 miles from Ice Lake with a 335-ft. elevation gain.

From the lake enjoy fine views of Fuller Peak, Vermillion Peak and Golden Horn. An old metal-sided mining cabin still stands beside the lake.

Driving Directions

From Silverton: From the intersection of Highway 550 and the turnoff to Silverton (110), drive 1.9 miles north on Highway 550 to County Road 7. Turn left on County Road 7 (signed for the South Mineral Campground) and follow this good gravel road for 4.4 miles to the trailhead parking area on the north side of the road (right) across from the South Mineral Campground.

From Ouray: Follow Highway 550 south from Ouray for 19.6 miles to CR 7. (The distance from Ouray is measured from the bottom of the switchback exiting the south end of town.) Make a sharp right onto County Road 7 (signed for the South Mineral Campground) and follow this good gravel road for 4.4 miles to the trailhead parking area on the north side of the road (right) across from the South Mineral Campground. If you reach Silverton you missed the turn.

10. Columbine Lake and Pass ★★★★★
Distance: 7.0 - 8.9 miles (RT)

This little known hike climbs steeply through forest and beautiful alpine meadows to a stunning glacial lake set amid rugged 13,000-ft. peaks. Panoramic views from nearby Columbine Pass encompass Bridal Veil basin and the Sneffels Range.

Distance: 7.0 miles (RT) to Columbine Lake
8.9 miles (RT) to Columbine Pass
Elevation: 10,346-ft. at Trailhead
12,693-ft. at Columbine Lake
13,094-ft. at Columbine Pass
Elevation Gain: 2,347-ft. to Columbine Lake
2,748-ft. to Columbine Pass

Difficulty: moderate-strenuous
Basecamp: Silverton, Ouray
Area: San Juan NF
Best Season: July - September
USGS Map(s): Ophir, Silverton

Why Hike Columbine Lake

Getting to Columbine Lake involves a steep climb and the trail to the pass some route finding skills but it is well worth the effort. The trail is truly off the beaten path, providing a degree of solitude not often found in such a beautiful location just 3.5 miles from a trailhead.

The strenuous hike to the lake traverses dense forest and gorgeous alpine meadows with see forever views. Columbine Lake, a turquoise jewel, is tucked in a stunning glacial bowl ringed by rugged ridges and peaks over 13,000-ft.

For hikers with the time and energy a side trip to Columbine Pass is highly recommended. The pass is located on the ridge to the northwest of the lake. Views from the pass extend west encompassing Bridal Veil basin, Mt Sneffels (14,150-ft.) and the Sneffels Range.

Trailhead to Columbine Lake

Distance from Trailhead to Columbine Lake: 7.0 miles (RT)
Elevation Columbine Lake: 12,693-ft.
Elevation Gain from Trailhead: 2,347-ft.

The Columbine Lake hike wastes no time gaining elevation. From the trailhead marked by a blaze on a tree (see driving directions), the trail ascends steep switchbacks through spruce-fir forest. After climbing 1.3 miles and gaining over 1,100-ft. the grade abates at bit and the trees thin. Views open to a narrow alpine basin carpeted in meadows sprinkled with wildflowers.

After leaving the last of the trees behind the steep climb resumes up the middle of the basin. Be sure to turn around and enjoy ever improving views of the high peaks rise above the east side of Highway 550.

At the head of the basin the trail makes a wide arc, swinging left (southwest) and then right (north), climbing through rocky meadows and scree to reach a saddle on a ridge at 12,541-ft., about 2.0 miles from the trailhead. Turn around just before reaching the saddle and check out the nice views to the east/southeast of Ohio Peak (12,673), Anvil Mountain (12,537-ft.) and Storm Peak (13,487-ft.).

The worst of the climbing is now over. The trail drops off the saddle and curves to the left (west), entering the Mill Creek drainage. Looking to the northeast on a clear day you will see the tips of the fourteeners in the Uncompahgre Wilderness. Below is the Chattanooga Loop on Highway 550.

The trail traverses meadows and passes a few small tarns, climbing gently as it contours beneath the ridge defining the basin's southern wall. Views extend across the basin to the peaks and ridges to the north and west.

At 2.4 miles (about 0.2 miles from the saddle), the trail reaches a "Y" intersection at a small rock cairn. At the cairn a faint trail branching right (northwest) toward Columbine Pass drops down into the drainage, crosses a stream (Mill Creek) and then climbs the hillside above Mill Creek, heading for the obvious saddle (Columbine Pass) on the ridge. We bear left (west) on the trail to Columbine Lake. Ahead you will see two trails cutting across a scree slope. Both trails lead to the lake. Assuming the lower trail is snow free, follow that path as it contours around the scree pile and heads southwest, staying to left (east) of Columbine Lake's outlet stream.

The hillside you are climbing is steep enough that you will not see the lake until you are right on top of it. At the head of the outlet stream is a stone dam and the end of the trail.

Columbine Lake is a turquoise jewel set in a stunning glacial bowl ringed by rugged ridges and peaks over 13,000-ft. Lookout Peak (13,661-ft.) rises above the southwestern end of the lake. The lake's shoreline invites exploration, providing multiple perspectives on the surrounding peaks. After taking a break, return the way you came or hike to the pass.

Columbine Lake to Columbine Pass

Segment Stats: 0.9 miles (one-way) from Columbine Lake to Columbine **Pass with 401-ft. elevation gain**
Distance from Trailhead to Columbine Lake: 8.9 miles (RT)
Elevation at Columbine Pass: 13,054-ft.
Elevation Gain from Trailhead: 2,749-ft.

Columbine Pass is a recommended side trip for hikers with the time and energy. There is no established trail from the lake to the obvious pass, located on the ridge to the northwest of the lake, but route finding is fairly easy across the open country.

To reach the pass climb about 25-ft. to the top of the hillside running along the lake's north shore and walk northwest, paralleling the lake. Near the end of the lake turn north, making a wide arc around a small tarn in a depression. Continue heading north, ascending through rocky meadows and aiming for the obvious saddle (pass) on the ridge.

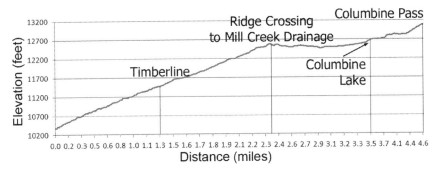

Along the way you may find a few faint trails but they do not last very long. Continue your ascent until you hit a trail coming down from the pass. (The trail is not very obvious and you may not hit it at all depending on the route you take to the saddle.) If you hit the trail turn left (northwest) and follow the path to the saddle at 13,080-ft. The total distance to the pass is just under 1 mile with a 400-ft. elevation gain.

From the top of the pass enjoy a bird's eye view into Bridal Veil basin on the west side of the pass. (A trail from the pass leads down to the basin and Lewis Lake (12,720-ft.). Mt. Sneffels (14,150-ft.) and the Sneffels Range dominate the view to the north/northwest. To the southeast are distant views of the high peaks of the Grenadier Range.

After taking in the panoramic views, retrace your steps back to the lake and then follow the trail back to the trailhead.

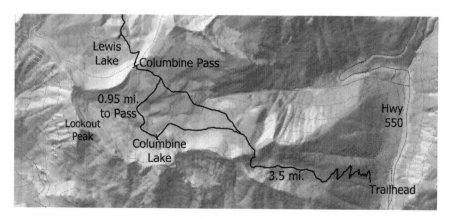

Driving Directions

From Silverton: Drive 4.8 miles north from Silverton on Highway 550 to the Ophir Pass Road (County Road 8) on the left. Turn left on the Ophir Pass road and follow it across a bridge. Shortly after crossing the bridge turn right on to Forest Road 820. Drive 0.7 miles to the trailhead located just beyond a wide part of the road. Park on your right at the wide spot and walk up the road (north) a brief distance to the trailhead marked by a blaze on a tree. Here an an obvious trail heads west uphill.

From Ouray: Drive 16 miles south of Ouray on Highway 550 (4.3 miles beyond Red Mountain Pass) and make a sharp right on (Forest Road 820),a gravel road. After the sharp right (essentially a hairpin curve off the highway) you will be on a gravel road heading north, paralleling the highway. Follow the road for a brief distance as it drops down to and cross the creek on a bridge. Beyond the bridge the road curves to the left (northwest) and climbs switchbacks up the hillside. Soon the road turns left (south) and levels out. Just pass a very narrow section of the road watch for a blaze on a tree to your right and a trail heading uphill (west) through the trees. Drive about 150-feet beyond the trailhead and park on the left at a wide spot in the road.

11. Porphyry Basin ★★★★★
Distance: 5.0 - 7.0 miles (RT)

This scenic hike climbs to two pretty lakes in gorgeous Porphyry Basin. Along the way the trail travels through wildflower-filled meadows and passes waterfalls, interesting rock formations and mining ruins. The lovely alpine meadows of the upper basin offer several options for off-trail exploration.

Distance: 5.0 miles (RT) to Bullion King Lake
6.4 miles (RT) to Porphyry Lake
7.0 miles (RT) to South Ridge Overlook
Elevation: 11,230-ft. at Trailhead
12,570-ft. at Bullion King Lake
12,800-ft. at Porphyry Lake
12,890-ft. at South Ridge Overlook
Elevation Gain: 1,340-ft. to Bullion King Lake
1,570-ft. to Porphyry Lake
1,660-ft. to South Ridge Overlook

Difficulty: moderate
Basecamp: Silverton, Ouray
Area: San Juan NF
Best Season: July - September
USGS Map(s): Telluride, Ironton

Why Hike Porphyry Basin

Typically I am not a big fan of walking jeep roads, but I make an exception when it comes to Porphyry Basin. This scenic, off-the-beaten path hike ascends to Bullion King Lake nestled in the stunningly beautiful Porphyry Basin. The initial segment follows a lightly trafficked dirt road and then a trail, traveling through beautiful wildflower-filled meadows and passing pretty waterfalls, interesting rock formations and remnant of old mines.

Beyond the lake faint trails and some route finding leads to the upper basin where lovely Porphyry Lake lies cradled beneath Three Needles Peak (13,481-ft.). The upper basin's open alpine meadows invite exploration. Off-trail routes climbing to saddles on the ridges to the north and west of Porphyry Lake offer terrific views into Bridal Veil Basin. Hikers ascending the route to the ridge crest rimming the south side of the basin are rewarded with a panorama of peaks extending from the Needles in the Grenadier Range in the southeast to the high peaks of the Uncompahgre Wilderness to the northeast.

Trailhead to Bullion King Lake

Distance from Trailhead: 5.0 miles (RT)
Ending/Highest Elevation: 12,570-ft.
Elevation Gain: 1,340-ft.

Note: This hiking description starts at the first parking area, which can be accessed by 2WD passenger vehicles if driven carefully (see driving directions below). Even with a 4WD I start from this spot since it allows for a longer walk. If you prefer to continue driving up the dirt road to the second parking area subtract one mile from the one way distances listed in the description below.

From the first parking area follow the jeep road as it climbs on moderately-easy grades up the hillside along the north side of Porphyry Gulch. Along the way enjoy views that extend south toward Bear (12,987-ft.), Sultan (13,368-ft.) and Anvil (12,537-ft.) mountains. McMillian Peak (12,804-ft.) and Red Mountain massif (12,890-ft.) rise above the Mineral Creek valley to the east. As you gain height, the summits of the high peaks in the Uncompahgre Wilderness appear above the sea of peaks and ridges to the northeast.

Pass two jeep roads branching to the right at 0.6 miles and 1.0 mile. Both roads lead to the Bear Basin road to the north. You will now see a few places to park off the road. This is the second parking area described in the "Driving Directions" below.

At 1.1 miles the road turns sharply to the left (west/southwest) and passes a sign warning of the rough and dangerous road ahead. Here the road narrows and starts climbing along a narrow, rocky shelf with steep drop-offs.

Soon the road rounds a bend and gorgeous Porphyry Basin springs into view. Three Needles (13,481-ft.) and Peak 13375 form the backdrop for basin to the west. Meadows sprinkled with wildflowers grow amid rock outcroppings and walls that define the basin's three levels. Waterfalls cascade down crevasses and over rock walls into Porphyry Gulch below the trail. The high peaks of the Grenadier Range rise in the distance to the southeast.

The grade abates briefly as the road crosses a slide area and then continues climbing the scenic basin. In season the slopes along both sides of the road are clad in wildflower-filled meadows.

At 1.8 miles the wood remains of an old mining structure appear to the left (south) of the trail. Soon the road crosses a creek and curves to the left (south) near a very large tailings pile. Walk through a parking area used by high clearance, 4WD vehicles. Past this point the road is closed to vehicular traffic. At the south end of the parking area a hillside covered in dirt now blocks the road. This is the site of mine waste repository constructed as part of a 2015 mine reclamation project.

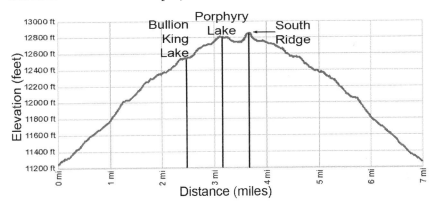

Walk straight ahead (south) across the dirt hillside to the continuation of the old mining road, marked by a row of boulders, and follow the road as it heads west on easy grades. At 2.1 miles the road curves to the left (east) and crosses second stream.

Beyond the stream the road/trail climbs a series of switchbacks on moderate grades. At the top of the switchbacks is a large boulder with an old sign indicating where vehicles had to stop prior to the reclamation project. Skirt the boulder and follow the old road, which is faint in spots, as it swings right (west) and ascends to the middle basin, passing a small tarn along the way.

Reach Bullion King Lake (12,570-ft.) at 2.5 miles. The west side of this pretty lake is ringed by rugged cliffs. A waterfall, which can't be seen from the southeast end of the lake, tumbles down a crevasse in the cliff face. Three Needles, Peak 13,375 and the rugged ridge between the two peaks tower above the lake to the west.

The lake is a great spot to take a break and laze in the sun. When you are done enjoying the lake either return to the trailhead for a 5.0 mile round trip hike or continue to Porphyry Lake. If time and energy permit, I strongly suggest hiking to the Porphyry Lake and exploring the upper basin.

To Porphyry Lake

Segment Stat: 0.7 miles (one-way) with a 230-ft. elevation gain
Distance from Trailhead: 6.4 miles (RT)
Ending/Highest Elevation: 12,800-ft.
Elevation Gain: 1,570-ft.

To find the trail to Porphyry Lake, cross Bullion King's outlet stream (the South Fork of Porphyry Creek) and then walk east along the north side of the stream for about 130-ft. A wide point on the outlet stream marks where the old mining road crosses the creek. Look left (north) across the meadows. You should be able to see faint vehicle tracks climbing the right (northeast) side of the bench rising to the north of the lake. Walk north across the meadows to where you can see the tracks and then climb the vehicle tracks on moderately steep grades to the top of the bench. As you crest the bench (2.7 miles) the grade abates and the trail curves to the left (west/northwest).

Snow cover may make seeing/finding the old road difficult. If snow is covering the trail, walk north across the meadows and then climb up the northeast end of the bench. At the top of the bench you should be able to see vestiges of the old track.

Continue following the old vehicle tracks across the bench on easy grades. At 2.8 mile the tracks curves to the left (south/southwest) and crosses a stream. The vehicle tracks are faint just before the crossing. This area is often covered in snow early in the season, which complicates route finding. On the other side of the creek the tracks, which head south/southwest are easier to follow.

Soon the old road curves to the right (west/northwest) and soon arrives at a small tailings pile and the ruins of a wooden structure at 3.0 miles. This is the site of the Porphyry Mine. Here the old road ends. After exploring the area around the mine walk west/southwest to pretty, unnamed lake (12,760-ft.) located a short distance from the mine.

To reach Porphyry Lake walk to inlet stream at the north end of the unnamed lake and follow the stream uphill (northwest), staying on the right (east) side of the stream. Note: there may not be any water in the stream but the stream course is evident, a small gully running between two low hills. As the stream bed peters out continue climbing northwest. You will soon crest a hill and see beautiful Porphyry Lake (12,800-ft.) nestled in a bowl beneath Three Needles. The distance from the mine to Porphyry Lake is just under 0.2 miles.

From the lake you can either retrace your steps to Bullion King Lake (11,230-ft.) and the trailhead for a 6.4 miles round trip hike or extend the hike by trying one of the off trail options listed below.

Side Trip to South Ridge Overlook

Distance from Porphyry Lake to the South Ridge: 0.6 miles (one-way) with a 135-ft. elevation gain
Distance from Trailhead: 7.0 miles (RT)
Ending/Highest Elevation: 12,890-ft.
Elevation Gain: 1,660-ft.

The easiest option for extending your hike is to climb the ridge rimming the south side of Porphyry Basin. To reach the ridge from Porphyry Lake, retrace your steps to the unnamed lake and then walk south along the lake's east shore. At the south end of the unnamed lake rock hop across a stream and then start climbing up a rocky slope, heading for the grassy slopes leading to the top of the ridge. You will pass a small lake on your left (east) as you start the climb.

The climb from the south end of the unnamed lake to the top of the ridge will gain about 135-ft. in less than 0.2 miles. From the top of the ridge enjoy terrific views of the sea of peaks extending from the Needles in the Grenadier Range to the southeast to the high peaks of the Uncompahgre wilderness to the northeast.

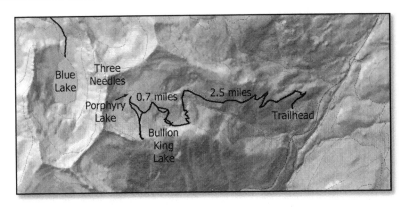

Side Trips to Mud and Blue Lake Overlooks

Mud Lake Overlook

Distance from Porphyry Lake to Mud Lake Overlook: 0.35 miles (one-way) with a 160-ft. elevation gain
Distance from Trailhead: 7.1 miles (RT)
Ending/Highest Elevation: 12,960-ft.
Elevation Gain from Trailhead: 1,730-ft.

Looking north from Porphyry Lake you will see a saddle on the low point of the ridge extending northeast from Three Needles to Peak 13477. This is what I call the Mud Lake Overlook. A snow cornice often last well into the season atop the saddle.

To reach the saddle walk around the east side of Porphyry Lake and then pick the route of least resistance to climb the talus slopes up to the saddle. Skirt the snow cornice, if present, to the left. The scenic saddle (12,960-ft.) is about 0.75 miles from the lake and overlooks Mud Lake and the Mud Lake Basin. In the distance to the northwest are nice views of the peaks rising above the north side of the Telluride Valley. La Junta peaks towers above the west side of Bridal Veil Basin.

Blue Lake Overlook

Distance from Porphyry Lake to Blue Lake Overlook: 0.4 mile (one-way) with a 460-ft. elevation gain
Distance from Trailhead: 7.2 miles (RT)
Ending/Highest Elevation: 13,260-ft.
Elevation Gain from Trailhead: 2,030-ft.

To the west of Porphyry Lake is a small saddle on the ridge running south from Three Needles. This is a much steeper and more difficult climb than the Mud Lake Overlook. I only recommend this option to experienced, well acclimated hikers who are comfortable climbing steep talus slopes. It is not a good option is snow covers the route.

To reach the saddle, skirt the south side of Porphyry Lake and the start climbing the steep grassy slopes beneath the saddle. About two-thirds of the way up the grass gives way to talus. This is a hard climb for most people. Members of your party may be uncomfortable with the steep pitch. I strongly recommend trekking poles on the descent.

Hikers reaching the saddle (13,260-ft.) are rewarded with great views Blue Lake in Bridal Veil's East Basin. La Junta Peak rises beyond the basin to the west while the peaks towering above Telluride fill the skyline to the northwest

Driving Directions

Driving directions from Silverton: From the intersection of Main Street and US 550 in Silverton, head north on US 550 N for 9.1 miles and turn left (west) on Forest Service Road 822. You can't see the road number from the highway but you will pass a marker a short distance up the road to verify you are in the right track.

The beginning of the road is in good condition but is narrow and steep to the first parking area. Beyond that point the road gets rougher to the second recommended parking area. Past this point you will soon see a sign warning of a rough and dangerous road ahead. This section of the road travels along a very narrow shelf with steep drop-offs and a few rock hills to climb. Passing another car along this road segment is not an option.

To reach the first parking area drive up the road for 0.7 miles. Before coming to the end of the first switchback you will see a road branching off to the left (south) that leads to a house. Ignore this road and continue up a series of switchbacks, passing a second road branching off to the left (south) to a second house at the top of the fifth switchback. Beyond this point you will soon see a good parking area on the left (south) side of the road below a cluster of spruce trees. This is the first parking area, recommended for people looking for a longer walk or drivers that don't feel comfortable proceeding further up the road.

To reach the second parking area, continue up the road another mile, passing two roads branching off to the right. Between the second road and a cluster of spruce trees you will find several places to park. This is the second parking area, located 1.7 miles from US 550.

High clearance, 4WD vehicle can continue beyond this point for another 0.9 miles to a parking area at the end of the road area near mining debris and a huge mound of mine tailings.

High clearance AWD or 4WD is recommended to the first two parking areas but a passenger vehicle, if driven carefully, can make it to the first parking area under good conditions. If driving a 2WD passenger vehicle, I strongly recommend checking on the current road conditions at the tourist offices in Ouray or Silverton.

Driving directions from Ouray: From Main Street and 6th Avenue in Ouray, drive 13 miles south on US 550 to Red Mountain Pass. Proceed down the south side of the pass for 0.7 miles and turn right (west) on Forest Service Road 822. This will be the first right turn after you pass the road to Black Bear Pass (FSR 823) on the right. You can't see the road number from the highway but you will pass a marker a short distance up the road to verify you are in the right track.

The beginning of the road is in good condition but is narrow and steep to the first parking area. Beyond that point the road gets rougher to the second recommended parking area. Past this point you will soon see a sign warning of a rough and dangerous road ahead. This section of the road travels along a very narrow shelf with steep drop-offs and a few rock hills to climb. Passing another car along this road segment is not an option.

To reach the first parking area drive up the road for 0.7 miles. Before coming to the end of the first switchback you will see a road branching off to the left (south) that leads to a house. Ignore this road and continue up a series of switchbacks, passing a second road branching off to the left (south) to a second house at the top of the fifth switchback. Beyond this point you will soon see a good parking area on the left (south) side of the road below a cluster of spruce trees. This is the first parking area, recommended for people looking for a longer walk or drivers that don't feel comfortable proceeding further up the road.

To reach the second parking area, continue up the road another mile, passing two roads branching off to the right. Between the second road and a cluster of spruce trees you will find several places to park. This is the second parking area located 1.7 miles from US 550.

High clearance, 4WD vehicle can continue beyond this point for another 0.9 miles to a parking area at the end of the road near mining debris and a huge mound of mine tailings.

High clearance AWD or 4WD is recommended to the first two parking areas but a passenger vehicle, if driven carefully, can make it to the first parking area under good conditions. If driving a 2WD passenger vehicle, I strongly recommend checking on the current road conditions at the tourist offices in Ouray or Silverton.

12. Highland Mary Lakes ★★★★★
Distance: 6.6 - 7.8 miles (RT)

A great hike to pretty lakes set amid scenic alpine meadows with wonderful views. An optional extension following a short section of the Continental Divide turns this out and back trail into a loop hike with extended views of the surrounding area.

Distance: 6.6 miles (RT) to Highland Mary Lakes
7.8 miles (loop) with Continental Divide extension
Elevation: 10,750-ft. at Trailhead
12,310-ft. at Highland Mary Lakes
12,630-ft. with Continental Divide extension
Elevation Gain: 1,560-ft. to Highland Mary Lakes
1,880-ft. with Continental Divide extension

Difficulty: moderate-strenuous
Basecamp: Silverton, Ouray
Area: Weminuche Wilderness, San Juan NF
Best Season: July - September
USGS Map(s): Howardsville

Why Hike Highland Mary Lakes

Reaching the trails traversing the spectacular high alpine tundra of the Weminuche Wilderness usually requires a multi-day backpacking trip. The Highland Mary Lakes trail is an exception, providing day hikers quick access to this alpine wonderland.

The hike visits three of the seven Highland Mary Lakes as well as the Verde Lakes, all above 12,000-ft. Getting to the lakes basin requires a bit of effort. The trail climbs over 1,300-ft. in 2 miles through a diverse landscape of trees, willows and meadows interspersed with picturesque waterfalls to reach the high lakes plateau.

Upon arriving at the Highland Mary Lakes hikers are greeted with breathtaking views of the glistening lakes set amid a broad expanse of rolling sub-alpine tundra. A gentle climb through the tundra leads to Verde Lakes and wonderful views of the Grenadier Range punctuated by the distinctive pyramid-shaped Vestal and Arrow Peaks.

The hike can be done as an out-and-back or turned into a loop by following a short section of the Continental Divide Trail with extended views of the surrounding area.

Trailhead to Verde Lakes

Distance from Trailhead: 6.6 miles (RT)
Elevation Verde Lake: 12,310-ft.
Elevation Gain: 1,560-ft.

The Highland Mary Lake trails starts just beyond the 4WD parking lot at a sign with a large map of the Weminuche Wilderness. (See driving directions below.) Before this sign there is an old wood sign pointing left (east) to the Continental Divide Trail (CDT) -- aka the Cunningham Gulch trail -- and right (south) for the Highland Mary Lakes.

The Highland Mary Lakes trail wastes no time gaining elevation, ascending on moderately-steep grades through meadows and forest, staying to the left (east) of Cunningham Creek. Just beyond a waterfall reach a junction (0.2 miles) pointing left to the CDT and straight ahead for the Highland Mary Lakes trail. The trail to the left provides alternative access to the Cunningham Gulch trail.

The trail becomes rougher as it climbs, occasionally crossing minor creeks with pretty waterfalls along the way. An open area by one of the falls provides nice views to the north.

After climbing for about 35 minutes (1.2 miles) and gaining 860-ft., the trail cross to the right (west) side of the creek and ascends steeply up a small cliff. Trees give way to a picturesque basin with diverse ground cover and small copses of trees set amid rocky knobs. Follow the trail as it heads west through the basin and climbs a minor drainage, staying to the right (north) of the creek.

Soon the route turns south again, ascending a steep slope beside the stream. At the base of the talus field the trail forks. Either trail will get you to your destination.

The trail to the left climbs steeply up the drainage, hugging the right (west side) of the creek. About halfway up the hill rock cairns mark a crossing to the left (east side) of the creek for the remainder of the climb. The trail to the right climbs a talus field, making a wide swing to the west of the creek drainage and then crosses a small boulder field to meet the first trail.

A short distance beyond where the two trails meet the first Highland Mary Lake (12,080-ft.) pops into view (2 miles and 1,330-ft. gain from the trailhead). The second lake is soon seen on the right (south) as the trail crosses the narrow strip of land separating the two lakes. This is a great spot for a rest with wonderful views to the north of the peaks lining Cunningham Gulch.

Continue the hike by following the trail as it swings around the left (eastern) side of the second lake. Soon views open to the left (east) to the third and largest of the Highland Mary lakes.

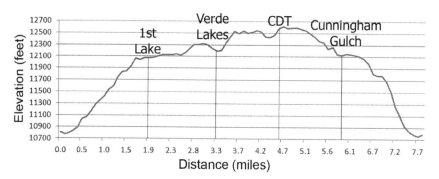

At the top of the third lake the path drops into a marshy area and becomes a little hard to follow as it crosses the lake's inlet stream. To stay on track, look for wooden post on the hillside above the marsh. As you head toward the post the continuation of the trail becomes evident in the boot beaten grass to the left of the post.

A second wooden post in the distance will help you navigate the path as it climbs gently south across the beautiful alpine meadows. The open landscape offers great views of the surrounding peaks and ridges.

From the inlet stream of the third lake the trail ascends a total of 215-ft. in 0.6 miles to a view point overlooking Verde Lakes (12,186-ft.) at 3.3 miles. To the south the Grenadier Range, with the distinctive pyramid-shaped Vestal and Arrow Peaks, rises above the lake.

Although this is a turnaround point for the out-and-back hike, the open alpine tundra invites exploration. A quick look at the map will show a number of smaller lakes within the vicinity worth visiting. Be sure to keep an eye on the weather. This is not a great place to be caught in a thunderstorm.

Loop Option with Continental Divide Extension

Segment Stat: Loop with the Continental Divide extension adds 1.2 miles with a 320-ft. elevation gain
Distance: 7.8 miles (loop)
Maximum Elevation: 12,630-ft.
Elevation Gain on the Loop: 1,880-ft.

If you wish to do the loop hike, look up the hillside to the left (east) from the Verde Lakes overlook and locate wooden posts marking the trail to the Continental Divide. Climb the hill, following the posts until an obvious trail appears. On the ascent be sure to turn around and enjoy views of the Grenadiers with Trinity, Vestal and Arrowhead Peaks, easy to pick out on the skyline.

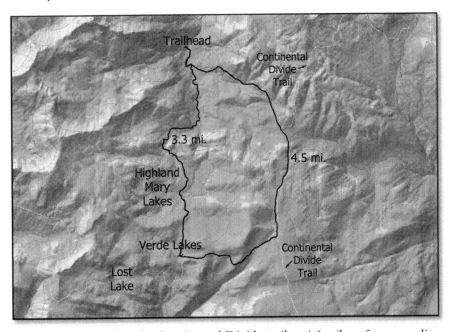

The trail reaches the Continental Divide trail at 4.6 miles after ascending over 320-ft. in 1.3 miles. Turn left (north) and follow the trail as it traverses rolling terrain along a beautiful meadow-clad plateau for 1.4 miles to wooden posts and a large rock cairn marking the junction with the Cunningham Gulch trail at 6.0 miles. Turn left on the Cunningham Gulch trail, which drops steeply down the west side of the divide, losing 1,350-ft. in 1.6 miles. Along the way you will reach an unmarked fork. The right fork leads to the trailhead with the old wooden sign seen just before the start of the Highland

Mary Lakes trail while the left branch hits the Highland Mary Lakes trail 0.2 miles above the trailhead. Either path will return you to the trailhead.

Driving Directions

From Silverton: Head northeast through Silverton on Greene Street, the town's main street. Pass the courthouse and bear right on County Road 2 to Howardsville (4 miles from the intersection). The road is paved for the first 2-miles and then turns to a good gravel surface. Turn right on County Road 4 (marked with a sign for the Old One Hundred Mine Tour). Follow CR 4, a good dirt road, for 3.7 miles up Cunningham Gulch to the ruins of a mine.

The road now becomes rougher (but still OK for 2WD vehicles), dropping down and crossing the creek on a bridge. On the other side of the creek the road starts climbing the right (west) side of the creek with the aid a long switchback. Follow the road for a little over 1.5 miles to an intersection with a road splitting off to the left. If you are in a 2WD, drive past this intersection to an obvious parking area on your left. Those with 4WD can turn left, following the road downhill and across the creek. The trailhead parking lot is just beyond the crossing.

From Ouray: Follow U.S. Highway 550 South from Ouray for 29 miles to the turnoff to Silverton and then follow the Silverton directions to the trailhead.

13. Crater Lake ★★★★★
Distance: 11.0 - 11.8 miles (RT)

A scenic hike to a pretty lake nestled beneath North Twilight Peak (13,075). The hike can be extended to the saddle beyond the lake and/or a scramble to the top of North Twilight.

Distance: 11.0 miles (RT) to Crater Lake
11.8 miles (RT) to Saddle above Crater Lake
Elevation: 10,770-ft. at Trailhead
11,640-ft. at Crater Lake
11,770-ft. at Saddle above Crater Lake
Elevation Gain: 870-ft. to Crater Lake
1,000-ft. to Saddle above Crater Lake
Difficulty: easy-moderate

Basecamp: Silverton, Ouray
Area: Weminuche Wilderness, San Juan NF
Best Season: July - September
USGS Map(s): Snowden Peak

Why Hike Crater Lake

The hike to Crater Lake does not require a big expenditure of energy for its scenic rewards. Starting at 10,770-ft. the trail traverses a rolling terrain of meadows and forests with great views of the surrounding peaks, gaining a net 1,300-ft. in 5.5 miles.

The lake, cradled in a pretty timber-lined bowl, is a photographer's delight with North Twilight Peak (13,075), rising to the south, reflected in its still waters.

Any easy side trip takes hikers to a panoramic saddle above the lake. From the saddle, a class 3 scramble up the east ridge of North Twilight Peak provides bird's eye views of the Needle Mountains and the Grenadier Range to the east.

Crater Lake is located in the rugged West Needle Mountains, an area added to the Weminuche Wilderness Area in 1993. This is the only trail penetrating this segment of the wilderness.

Trailhead to Crater Lake

Distance from Trailhead: 11.0 miles (RT)
Elevation: 11,640-ft.
Elevation Gain: 870-ft.

In 1993 Congress expanded the Weminuche Wilderness to include the rugged West Needle Mountains, wedged between a deep gorge of the Animas River and Lime Creek south of Molas Pass. Only one trail, Crater Lake, penetrates this segment of the wilderness.

The hike to Crater Lake starts at pretty Andrews Lake, a popular fishing spot just south of Molas Pass (see driving directions below). Starting at the southwest end of the parking area the trail skirts the west shore of the lake, crosses a meadow and ascends a tree covered hillside on switchbacks, gaining 450-ft. in 1.2 miles. This is the steepest climb of the hike.

Views from the meadows around Andrews, along with intermittent views from openings in the trees while climbing the hillside, include West Turkshead (12,849-ft.) and Grand Turk (13,180-ft.) to the north, Twin Sisters (13,432 and 13,372) and Jura Knob (12,594) rising on the ridge to the west and Snowdon Peak to the southeast.

From the top of the hill the trail drops 240-feet into a drainage traversing pretty meadows with pockets of Engelmann Spruce and firs. A second climb gains 370-ft. reaching the top of a hill at 2.4 miles.

Beyond the second climb the trail ascends on easy to moderate grades through meadows and forests for the next 1.6 miles, gaining 400-ft. Openings offer great views of Engineer Mountain (12,968-ft.), Jura Knob and Twin Sisters to the west. As the trail swings east views open to North Twilight Peak (13,075) to the south.

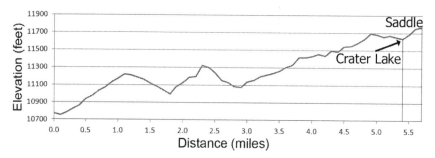

At 4.0 miles the path enters heavy timber and stays in the woods for the next 1.1 miles. At 5.1 miles the trail drops into a small depression, skirts a marshy area to your left (east), and then climbs over a hill to the basin holding Crater Lake (11,640-ft.) at 5.5 miles. North Twilight Peak, rising to the southwest, forms the perfect backdrop for this pretty lake ringed by a forest.

Photographers will snap plenty of pictures of North Twilight Peak reflected in the lake's still waters. Fishermen may want to try their luck at catching some of the lake's cutthroat trout. Numerous camping areas are evident in the trees to the north and west of the lake.

Crater Lake to the Saddle

Segment Stat: 0.4 miles (one-way) from Crater Lake to the Saddle with a **130-ft. elevation gain**
Distance - Trailhead to the Saddle: 11.8 miles (RT)
Elevation at Saddle: 11,770-ft.
Elevation Gain - Trailhead to the Saddle: 1,000-ft.

For panoramic views of the peaks to the west and south of Molas Pass along with a restricted view the Needles, hike to the obvious saddle (11,770-

ft.) southwest of the lake. The faint trail swings around the east side of the lake and proceeds up a grassy slope, skirting rock piles and a small pond. Round trip to the saddle is 0.4 miles (RT) with a 130-ft. elevation gain.

When you are done enjoying the views, retrace your steps to return to the trailhead.

To climb North Twilight Peak (13,075-ft) proceeds west from the saddle, climbing the mountain's northeast shoulder and east ridge. The class 2-3 scramble requires a head for heights when crossing a narrow exposed ridge. Panoramic views from the top provide a bird's eye view of the Needles and the Grenadier Range to the east. Total elevation gain from the trailhead is 2,305-ft. Note: The climb to North Twilight Peak is recommended for experienced parties only.

Driving Directions

From Silverton: From the intersection of Main Street in Silverton (State Highway 110) and U.S. 550, drive south on U.S. 550 for 7.3 miles to the Andrews Lake Road. It is 6.4 miles to the top of Molas Pass. Andrews Lake Road is 0.94 miles beyond the pass. Turn left and drive a little over 0.5 mile on the narrow paved road to the parking area at Andrews Lake. The trailhead is located on the southwest end of the parking area.

Driving Directions from Ouray: Drive south on U.S. 550 for 30.7 miles to the Andrews Lake Road. Andrews Lake Road is 0.94 miles beyond Molas pass. Turn left and drive a little over 0.5 mile on the narrow paved road to the parking area at Andrews Lake. The trailhead is located on the southwest end of the parking area.

Driving directions from Durango: Drive 45-miles north of Durango on US 550 to the Andrews Lake turn off. The turn off is 6.6 miles beyond Coal Bank Pass and about 0.5 miles from the Lime Creek rest area. Turn right and drive a little over 0.5 mile on the narrow paved road to the parking area at the lake. The trailhead is located on the southwest end of the parking area.

14. Colorado Trail: Little Molas Lake to Lime Creek ★★★★☆

Distance: 7.4 - 10.1 miles (RT)

This relatively easy out-and-back hike on a segment of the Colorado Trail provides panoramic views from the high meadows above the West Lime Creek drainage.

Distance: 10.1 miles (RT) to Lime Creek Drainage
Elevation: 10,895-ft. at Trailhead 11,650-ft. at high point
Elevation Gain: 755-ft. at high point
Difficulty: easy-moderate

Basecamp: Silverton, Ouray
Area: San Juan NF
Best Season: July - September
USGS Map(s): Snowden Peak, Engineer Mountain

Why Hike the Colorado Trail from Little Molas Lake to Lime Creek

This relatively easy walk gives day hikers a scenic taste of the Colorado Trail, an epic 471-mile route stretching between Denver and Durango. The out-and-back hike follows a 5-mile segment of the trail, traversing pretty meadows with panoramic views high above the Lime Creek Drainage.

The hike is located just north of Molas Pass (10,910-ft.) in the area of the 1879 Lime Creek Burn that incinerated 26,000-acres of forest. The fire burned with such intensity that the forest has still not recovered.

Vast meadows, sprinkled with replanted lodgepole pines, now cover the area once blanketed with thick forest, offering far reaching vistas of the Grenadier Range to the east, the West Needle Mountains and Engineer Peak to the south and Twin Sisters to the west. West Turkshead Peak dominates the skyline to the north.

Trailhead to Lime Creek Drainage

From the trailhead at the western end of Little Molas Lake (see driving directions below), follow the Colorado Trail as it heads northwest climbing limestone terraces on switchbacks with moderately easy grades through pockets of trees and open meadows with views south to Engineer Peak (12,698-ft.) and North Twilight Peak (13,075-ft.).

After gaining 390-ft. in 1.3 miles the trail turns right (northeast) and joins a wide dirt track near the top of a ridge. The eroded track ascends to and traverses the ridge towards West Turkshead Peak (12,849-ft.). Along the way views open west to the Twin Sisters (13,432 and 13,374-ft.) and Jura Knob (12,592-ft.). Snowden Peak and the Grenadier Range beyond fill the skyline to the east.

Follow the track uphill for 0.7 miles. The trail narrows and turns left (northwest) as it nears West Turkshead Peak, two miles from the start of the hike.

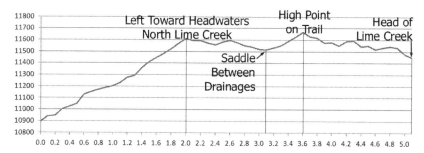

The trail now traverses the east side of the North Lime Creek drainage. Toward the head of the drainage the path descends to and crosses the saddle between Bear Creek (to the north) and North Lime Creek (to the south) at 3.1 miles. Views at the saddle extend north to Bear Mountain (12,987-ft.) and Sultan Mountain (13,368-ft.).

From the saddle the trail heads west, ascending to the high point of the hike (11,650-ft.) at 3.6-miles and then loses 100-ft. over 0.4 miles as it crosses and curves around the ridge separating the North Lime Creek and Lime Creek drainages. Below the trail two tarns lie nestled on the ridge's broad shoulder.

Continue walking until the trail starts to drop towards the head of Lime Creek on switchbacks. This is the 5 mile mark and a good place to turn around.

From this vantage point panoramic views encompass Twin Sisters, Jura Knob, Engineer Mountain, North Twilight Peak, the Snowden Mountains and the Grenadier Range. After taking a break and soaking in the scenery, retrace your steps enjoying the view all over again on the return leg.

Note: Mountain bikes are permitted on this trail.

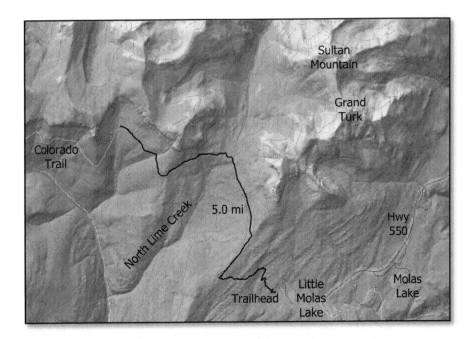

Driving Directions

From Silverton and Ouray: Go 5.5 miles south of Silverton (27 miles south of Ouray, 44.5 miles north of Durango) on US 550 and turn west on Little Molas Lake Road. The Molas Lake Road is 0.4 miles north of Molas Pass. Follow the road for 0.8 miles to the parking area beyond the lake. The Colorado Trail trailhead is located at the northwest end of the parking area.

15. Sneffels Highline ★★★★★
Distance: 8.0 - 12.7 miles (loop)

This is my favorite hike in Telluride, crossing a high saddle separating two gorgeous alpine basins. Along the way the trail traverses meadows filled with thigh-high wildflowers and serves up spectacular views of the high peaks surrounding the Telluride valley and the San Miguel Mountains in the Lizard Head Wilderness.

Distance: 12.7 miles (loop)
Elevation: 8,900-ft. at Trailhead
Maximum elevation: 12,280-ft.
Elevation Gain: 3,380-ft.
Difficulty: strenuous

Basecamp: Telluride
Area: Mt. Sneffels Wilderness, Uncompahgre NF
Best Season: July - September
USGS Map(s): Mt. Sneffels, Telluride

Why Hike the Sneffels Highline Trail

If I only had time for one hike in the Telluride area, I'd choose the Sneffels Highline. This classic loop hike, leaving right from town, features spectacular views, two beautiful alpine basins and pretty meadows with thigh-high fields of wildflowers.

Be forewarned the trail is strenuous, covering 12.7 miles and climbing 3,380-ft. to its high point on a saddle below Mt. Emma (12,280-ft.). Don't let the challenge deter you. Pick a beautiful day and get an early start so you can enjoy this premier hike at a leisurely pace.

Trailhead to Saddle

Distance from Trailhead: 8.0 miles (RT)
Highest Elevation: 12,280-ft.
Elevation Gain: 3,380-ft.

The Sneffels Highline loop starts and ends at the Jud Wiebe trail at the north end of Aspen Street in Telluride (see directions to the trailhead below). Completed in 1990, the trail combines existing routes with new trails to create one of the classic hikes in the San Juan Mountains.

Follow the Jud Wiebe uphill as it crosses a bridge and swings west, ascending on a broad track. As you climb views open to downtown Telluride and the ski area across the valley. Reach a trail junction at 0.8 miles after gaining 670-ft. and turn left on the Deep Creek (#418) trail. (The Jud Wiebe trail branches right at the junction.) Cross Butcher creek and, in about 300-ft., arrive at a second junction signed for the Sneffels Highline (#434) and Deep Creek.

I recommend hiking counter-clockwise, turning right (north) on the Highline Trail and returning via the Deep Creek Trail (to the left). While initially steeper, you will get over the high point in the trail early in the day before the onset of afternoon thunder storms, a frequent occurrence in the Rockies.

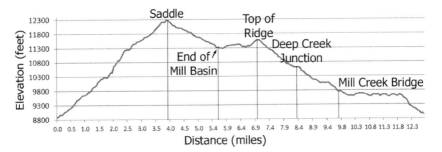

Follow the Highline as it climbs along the west side (left) of Butcher creek drainage, passing through stands of aspen, spruce-fir forest and small meadows. Switchbacks ease the moderately steep climb up the drainage.

About 40 minutes from the junction the trail breaks out of the trees and continues its ascent on switchbacks climbing through grassy meadows to a ridge. From the meadows enjoy views of the ski area and the rugged peaks defining the Bear Creek drainage across the valley. To the southwest the peaks of the San Miguel Mountains in the Lizard Head Wilderness, including Wilson Peak (14,017), Mount Wilson (14,246), El Diente Peak (14,159) and the distinctive profile of Lizard Head Peak (13,113), grace the skyline.

Beyond the meadows the trail continues climbing, passing through a notch to gain the west side of the ridge. Openings in the spruce-fir forest provide views of the steep, eroded hillside of the Pack Basin drainage to the west. A final set of switchbacks through a nice stand of spruce brings you to lower end of Pack Basin (11,750-ft.), a pretty alpine bowl carpeted with an emerald green meadow sprinkled with wildflowers.

The basin is cradled beneath the steep, jagged walls of Mt. Emma (13,581-ft.), rising above the head of the basin, and Greenback Mountain (12,976-ft.) to the south. Behind you are distant views of the San Miguel Range.

A narrow trail, marked by rock cairns, leads through the meadow to the head of the basin where a series of steep switchbacks climb the north wall of the bowl to a saddle (12,280-ft.) on the ridge extending west from Mt. Emma. The saddle, separating Pack and Mill Basins, is reached in just under 4-miles from the start of the hike.

The saddle offers panoramic views of the San Miguel Mountains and Lizard Head Wilderness to the southwest and the peaks rising above the Telluride Ski area to the south. Looking north beautiful Mill Creek Basin is nestled beneath a rugged ridge running between Gilpin Peak (13,694-ft.) and Dallas Peak (13,809-ft.).

Completing the Loop

Segment Stat: 8.7 miles (one-way) from the top of the saddle back to the trailhead
Total Distance for the Loop: 12.7 miles (loop)
Maximum Elevation: 12,280-ft.
Elevation Gain/Loss for the Loop: 3,380-ft. / -3,380-ft.

From the saddle the trail descends on rocky switchbacks to the head of the Mill Creek basin and then winds its way past a waterfall and down through meadows, staying to the right (north) of Mill Creek. During the height of wildflower season the trail travels through fields of waist-deep wildflowers at the lower end of the basin.

At the end of the basin the trail descends a series of short, tight switchbacks near a waterfall on Mill Creek and then contours along grassy slopes beneath Dallas Peak. After crossing a minor ridge the route climbs 200-ft. through intermittent pockets of trees to the ridge dividing the Mill and Eider Creek drainages. Along the way enjoy beautiful views of Mill Basin, the steep, colorful cliffs lining the east side of the Mill Creek drainage and ever expanding views of the high peaks to the south and east of Telluride.

From the top of the ridge the trail drops steeply on switchbacks through pretty stands of aspen to the Deep Creek Trail, losing 900-ft. in 1.3 miles. Turn left (east) on the Deep Creek trail and descend through meadows and trees to another set of steep switchbacks dropping to Mill Creek at 9,900-ft. At this point the trail meets a dirt road. A Deep Creek trail sign points left toward the Jud Wiebe trail and right (south) toward Mill Creek Road. Head left to complete the loop.

The trail soon crosses a bridge over Mill Creek and then heads south following a section of the Deep Creek trail locally referred to as the Waterline Trail because it follows an old water pipe. (Note mountain bikes are permitted on this section of the trail.) A little over a mile after the bridge the route crosses a ridge and turns left (east), heading back to the intersection with the Highline trail. From the intersection turn right to reach the Jud Wiebe trail leading back to town.

Total hiking time, including stops, is between 7.5 to 8 hours.

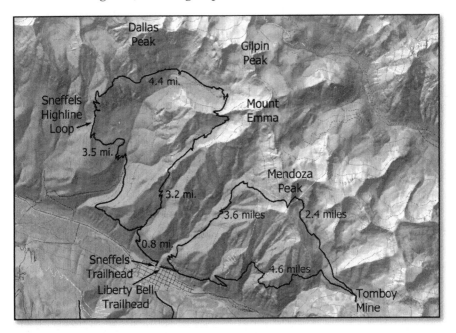

Driving Directions

Walking Directions in Telluride: From Telluride's main street (Colorado Avenue) turn north onto Aspen Street and proceed uphill past the last of the houses to the Jud Wiebe trailhead.

Parking in Telluride: Parking is by permit only at the trailhead and limited to two-hour parking along Colorado Avenue. Permits are required to park on most of the side streets around town.

Free day-use parking is available in Carhenge Lot, just off West Pacific Avenue at the west end of town near the base of Lift 7, or at the south end of Mahoney Drive, near the west entrance to town. A free shuttle bus, called the Galloping Goose, runs between the parking lots and various stops in downtown Telluride.

There is also free parking in the mountain village. From there you can take the free gondola into town and easily walk to the trailhead.

16. Lewis Lake and Mine ★★★★★

Distance: 8.0 - 8.8 miles (RT)

This scenic hike winding up Bridal Veil Basin past the historic Lewis Mill to Lewis Lake, nestled in a stark glacial basin at 12,700-ft. Along the way pass remnants of the area's rich mining history, numerous waterfalls and hillsides filled with spectacular wildflowers displays.

Distance: 8.0 miles (RT) to Lewis Mine
8.8 miles (RT) to Lewis Lake
Elevation: 10,400-ft. at Trailhead
12,448-ft. at Lewis Mine
12,700-ft. at Lewis Lake
Elevation Gain: 2,048-ft. to Lewis Mine
2,300-ft. to Lewis Lake

Difficulty: moderate-strenuous
Basecamp: Telluride
Area: Uncompahgre NF
Best Season: July - September
USGS Map(s): Telluride

Why Hike Lewis Lake and Mine

Pretty Bridal Veil Basin begins atop the headwall at the eastern end of the Telluride Valley. A seldom used mining road traverses the length of this hanging valley, leading to scenic glacial lake basins nestled in alpine meadows. Along the way the route passes remnants of the area's rich mining history, numerous waterfalls on Bridal Veil Creek and hillsides filled with spectacular wildflowers displays.

One of the best hikes in the area leads past the largely intact 5-story historic Lewis Mill (12,448-ft.) to Lewis Lake (12,700-ft.), set amid a magnificent alpine amphitheater in the upper basin. Beyond the lake a trail climbs to an unnamed pass with views of the Columbine Lake basin near Silverton and a panorama of peaks around the Telluride area.

Along the way to Lewis Lake you will pass the turn off to the Blue Lake trail, a great destination for hikers looking for a shorter day. The trail to Blue Lake, nestled in a stark glacial cirque scattered with mining debris, leads past the remains of an old tram, mining cabins and a bunkhouse. (See the Blue Lake hiking description for more information.)

Whatever your destination getting to the beginning of Bridal Veil basin is its own adventure. The 4WD road to the trailhead switchbacks up the headwall of Telluride's box canyon, providing terrific view of the town, Bridal Veil Falls and the historic power plant at the top of the falls.

Trailhead to the Lewis Lake Junction

Distance to Lewis Lake Junction: 6.2 miles (RT)
Elevation: 12,360-ft.
Elevation Gain: 1,960-ft.

A hiking trip to Bridal Veil Basin starts with a walk or a drive up the 4WD jeep road just past the Pandora Mill at the east end of Telluride. The road features stunning views of Bridal Veil Falls, Telluride and the restored historic power plant atop the falls.

Bridal Veil Falls, the tallest freefalling waterfall in Colorado, plunges 365-ft. from just beneath the power plant to headwaters of the San Miguel River. An excellent viewpoint at the base of the falls is located 1.2 miles up the jeep road at a hairpin curve on one of the switchbacks. The viewpoint is often enveloped in mist from the water thundering over the rock face and hitting a small pool at the base of the falls.

The walk or drive of the remaining 0.8 miles to the trailhead enjoys great views of the steep cliffs forming the head of the Telluride valley and the town in the distance. Along the way dramatic views open to the power plant perched on a ledge just above the falls. The building, restored in the 1990's, is listed on the National Register of Historic Places.

The power plant, the second oldest AC generation facility in the country, was built in 1907 to supply the Smuggler's Union Mine. Water driving the generators is piped from Blue Lake (see Blue Lake trail description).

If you plan to walk up the road add 4.0-miles to the round trip hiking distances and get an early start. Walking the road turns this into a 12.8-mile round trip hike to Lewis Lake gaining 3,680-ft. in elevation. For more details on walking the road see the Bridal Veil Falls trail description.

The trail into Bridal Veil Basin starts at a gate blocking vehicle access to the power plant. Duck through the opening in the gate and stay on the seldom used mining road as it swings to the left (south) and enters the basin. In a few minutes pass above the power plant building (on the right). The building and the area around the plant is private property.

Follow the rocky road as it ascends on moderate grades along the left (east) side of the creek, past picturesque cascades and waterfalls. Switchbacks ease the way up a few steep sections.

During mid-July to early-August the hillsides along the trail are awash in wildflowers. As you climb the trees thin and views open to the north (behind you) to the mountains forming the northern wall of the Telluride valley.

An unmarked intersection at 11,470-ft. is reached after walking 1.7 miles and gaining 1,072-ft. Continue straight ahead (the road on the right) toward Lewis Lake. The road to the left leads to Blue Lake. (See the Blue Lake description for more information.)

Stay on the road as it climbs through meadows, crosses streams and passes small tarns. Near the head of the basin two roads are seen in the distance climbing toward the ridge. The road on the left ascends to Columbine Pass above Lewis Lake while the road on the right heads to Ophir.

Reach a second junction at 3.1 miles after walking 1.4 miles and gaining about 900-ft. from the junction with the Blue Lake trail. Turn left to reach the Lewis Mill/Mine and Lewis Lake. (There is no trail sign at the intersection, just a post.) The trail to the right continues toward the head of the basin.

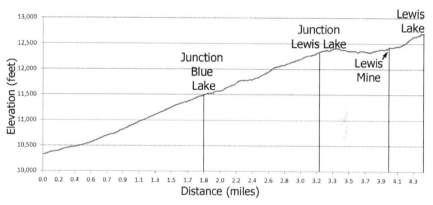

To the Lewis Mill

Segment Stats: 0.9 miles (one-way) with a 88-ft. elevation gain
Distance - Trailhead to Lewis Mill: 8.0 miles (RT)
Elevation Lewis Mill: 12,448-ft.
Elevation Gain - Trailhead to Lewis Mill: 2,048-ft.

Follow the trail as it heads southeast, traversing a rolling landscape of meadows and rock outcrops on easy grades. Upon reaching a creek (the outlet stream for Lewis Lake) the trail swings south, climbing along the right (west) side of the creek.

The Lewis Mill (12,448-ft.) is situated about 0.9-miles from the second junction on the left (east) side of the trail. A small cabin is located near the Mill and mining debris is scattered around the site.

The 5-story Mill, built in 1907, served as a 60-ton capacity ore-concentration facility in the early 1900's. Work in 2001 stabilized the structure and a new roof was added in 2006. The building, owned by San Miguel County, is listed the National Register of Historic Places.

To Lewis Lake

Segment Stats: 0.4 miles (one-way) with a 252-ft. elevation gain
Distance - Trailhead to Lewis Lake: 8.8 miles (RT)
Elevation Lewis Lake: 12,700-ft.
Elevation Gain - Trailhead to Lewis Lake: 2,300-ft.

Beyond the Mill the trail climbs a steep rocky drainage gaining 250-ft. in 0.4-miles to reach the dam at the end of Lewis Lake (12,700-ft) at 8.8 miles. The lake is set amid a large rocky basin surrounded on three sides with peaks towering above 13,000-ft.

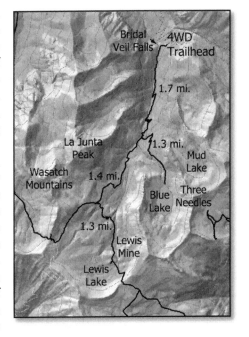

Hikers with the time and energy can follow the very rocky route climbing to Columbine Pass on the ridge to the southeast of the lake. The pass is about 0.5-miles from the lake and entails a climb of 380-ft. From the top of the pass you have a bird's-eye view of Columbine Lake to the south and the vast panorama of peaks surrounding Telluride.

After taking a break return the way you came, enjoying the wildflowers, waterfalls and scenic views of the mountains rising above Telluride.

Wasatch Trail Junction: The trail up Bridal Veil Basin links to the Wasatch trail in Bear Creek. At the junction with the Lewis Lake and Mine trail stay right (Lewis Lake and Mine are to the left) and follow the trail as it climbs in a southwest direction toward a scree covered hillside. The trail will cross the edge of the scree and head toward the head of the basin.

A junction is reached just before the head of the basin. The trail straight ahead leads to Ophir and the Blixt trail. Take the faint trail heading right (west), ascending to an obvious saddle. At the top of the saddle a trail is seen descending into the Bear Creek drainage. This is the Wasatch Trail that eventually meets with the Bear Creek trail that descends steeply to Telluride. (This is a VERY long loop and only recommended for experienced hikers!)

Driving Directions

From Telluride: Drive east through Telluride on Colorado Avenue for a little over 2.0 miles past the Pandora Mill to a large unmarked parking area. Park here if you are driving a 2WD vehicle. High clearance AWD or 4WD is recommended beyond this point.

If you are in a high clearance AWD / 4WD follow the dirt road, marked as Forest Road #636 on maps, for 2.0-miles up a series of switchbacks to the Bridal Veil Power plant. The road gets rougher and rockier as you climb.

Parking is VERY limited at the top and fills up early in the morning. Be sure not to block the gate. If there is no parking, turn around and go back down the road until you find a safe, wide spot along the road to park out of the flow of traffic (and not on private property.) A good place to park is at the base of the waterfall. From the waterfall walk 0.8-miles up the road.

Note: Two-way traffic is permitted between the Pandora Mine and the power plant. The road above the power plant, the notorious Black Bear Road, is one-way downhill toward Telluride. [The Black Bear road, starting south of Red Mountain Pass on Highway 550, goes over Black Bear Pass (12,840-ft.) and descends Ingram Basin on dangerous and difficult switchbacks to meet the 4WD road coming up from Telluride.]

17. Blue Lake (in Telluride) ★★★★★
Distance: 6.0 miles (RT)

This nice hike up pretty Bridal Veil Basin leads past waterfalls and wildflowers to Blue Lake (12,220-ft.) nestled in a glacial cirque littered with mining relics.

Distance: 6.0 miles (RT)
Elevation: 10,400-ft. at Trailhead
12,220-ft. at Blue Lake
Elevation Gain: 1,820-ft. to Blue Lake
Difficulty: moderate-strenuous

Basecamp: Telluride
Area: Uncompahgre NF
Best Season: July - September
USGS Map(s): Telluride
See Page 84 for Map

Why Hike Blue Lake Trail

Wildflowers and waterfalls abound on this pretty walk up Bridal Veil Basin to a large alpine lake set in a stark glacial cirque at 12,220-ft. Along the way the trail passes historic mining structures including the remains of an old tram, mining cabins and a bunkhouse. More mining debris is scattered around the lake.

Getting to the start of this hike is its own adventure. The 4WD road leading to the trailhead switchbacks up the headwall of Telluride's box canyon, providing terrific views of Telluride, Bridal Veil Falls -- Colorado's longest freefalling waterfall, and the historic power plant atop the falls.

Trailhead to turnoff to Blue Lake

Distance from Trailhead: 3.4 miles (RT)
Elevation: 11,472-ft.
Elevation Gain: 1,072-ft.

A hike to Bridal Veil Basin starts with a walk or a drive up the 4WD jeep road that starts just past the Pandora Mill at the east end of Telluride (see driving directions below). The road features stunning views of Bridal Veil Falls, Telluride and the restored historic power plant at the top of the falls.

Bridal Veil Falls, the tallest freefalling waterfall in Colorado, plunges 365-ft. from just beneath the power plant to a stream feeding the San Miguel River running through Telluride. An excellent viewpoint at the base of the falls is located 1.2 miles up the jeep road at a hairpin curve on one of the switchbacks. The viewpoint is often enveloped in mist from the water thundering over the rock face and hitting a small pool at the base of the falls.

Beyond the viewpoint it is a 0.8-mile walk or drive to the gate blocking further vehicle access and the start of the hike. This section of the road enjoys wonderful views of the steep cliffs forming the head of the Telluride valley and the town in the distance. Along the way dramatic views open to the power plant perched on a ledge just above the falls. The building, restored in the 1990's, is listed on the National Register of Historic places.

The power plant, the second oldest AC generation facility in the country, was built in 1907 to supply the Smuggler's Union Mine. Water driving the generators is piped from Blue Lake, our destination.

If you plan to walk up the road add 4.0-miles to the round trip hiking distances and get an early start. Walking the road turns this into a 10-mile round trip hike to Blue Lake gaining 3,200-ft. in elevation. For more details on walking the road see the Bridal Veil Falls trail description.

The trail into Bridal Veil Basin starts at the gate blocking vehicle access to the power plant. Duck through the gate and stay on the seldom used mining road as it swings to the left (south) and enters the basin. In a few minutes you will pass above the power plant building (on the right). The building and the area around the plant is private property.

Follow the rocky road as it ascends on moderate grades along the left (east) side of the creek, past picturesque cascades and waterfalls. Switchbacks help ease the way up a few steep sections.

During mid-July to early-August the hillsides along the trail are awash in wildflowers. As you climb the trees thin and views open to the north (behind you) to the mountains forming the northern wall of the Telluride valley.

An unmarked intersection is reached after walking 1.7 miles and gaining 1,072-ft. Ahead you will see the top of a distinctive pyramid shaped mountain peeking over the steep hillside. Turn left at the junction to reach Blue Lake. The road continuing straight ahead (the road on the right) leads to upper Bridal Veil basin and the turn off to the Lewis Mill and Lake. (See the Lewis Mill and Lake trail description for more information.)

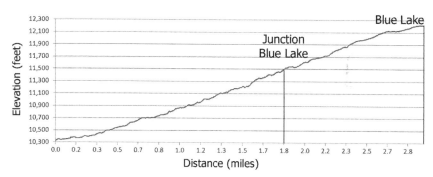

To Blue Lake

Segment Stat: 1.3 miles (one-way) with a 748-ft. elevation gain
Distance - Trailhead to Blue Lake: 6.0 miles (RT)
Elevation Blue Lake: 12,220-ft.
Elevation Gain - Trailhead to Blue Lake: 1,820-ft.

Beyond the turnoff the trail gets rougher as it ascends a few steep pitches. When you hit a second intersection go right. (Turning left leads to Mud Lake.)

Old tram towers and other evidence of past mining activity is evident along the trail. At 2.6-miles the trail reaches the top of a hill and passes an old wood building with a metal roof.

The grade abates and the trail now climbs gently towards the lake. Several wood mining buildings with metal siding and roofs are seen to the right (west) in the flower-filled meadow below the trail. (Stay on the road. The area around Blue Lake is private property.)

Straight ahead the craggy ridge forming the head of East Basin fills the skyline while to the west you will see La Junta Peak (13,472-ft.) and Wasatch Mountain (13,555-ft.).

Follow the road for another 0.4 miles as it winds through meadows to a rocky overlook above the lake. Blue Lake (12,220-ft.) lies nestled in a rocky East Basin surrounded by peaks towering over 13,000-ft. From this vantage point you can see pipes and other mining debris strewn around the lake.

After taking a break return the way you came, enjoying the wildflowers, waterfalls and views to the north of the peaks rising above the Telluride valley.

Driving Directions

From Telluride: Drive east through Telluride on Colorado Avenue for a little over 2.0 miles past the Pandora Mill to a large unmarked parking area. Park here if you are driving a 2WD vehicle. High clearance AWD / 4WD is recommended beyond this point.

If you are in a high clearance AWD/4WD follow the dirt road, marked as Forest Road #636 on maps, for 2.0-miles up a series of switchbacks to the Bridal Veil Power plant. The road gets rougher and rockier as you climb.

Parking is VERY limited at the top and fills up early in the morning. Be sure not to block the gate. If there is no parking, turn around and go back down the road until you find a safe, wide spot along the road to park out of the flow of traffic and not on private property. A good place to park is at the base of the waterfall. From the waterfall walk 0.8-miles up the road.

Note: Two-way traffic is permitted between the Pandora Mine and the power plant. The road above the power plant, the notorious Black Bear Road, is one-way downhill toward Telluride. [The Black Bear road, starting south of Red Mountain Pass on Highway 550, goes over Black Bear Pass (12,840-ft.) and descends Ingram Basin on dangerous and difficult switchbacks to meet the 4WD road coming up from Telluride.]

18. Bridal Veil Falls ★★★★★
Distance: 4.0 miles (RT)

This hike, ascending a jeep road, offers stunning views of Bridal Veil Falls, the tallest freefalling waterfall in Colorado, the historic power plant at the top of the falls and the Telluride valley. The views are an added bonus for hikers who walk or drive up the road to reach the Bridal Veil trailhead leading to Blue Lake, Lewis Lake and other destinations in the Bridal Veil basin.

Distance: 4.0 miles (RT)
Elevation: 9,020-ft. - Trailhead
10,400-ft. at Bridal Veil Falls
Elevation Gain: 1,380-ft.
Difficulty: moderate

Basecamp: Telluride
Area: Uncompahgre NF
Best Season: July - September
USGS Map(s): Telluride

Trailhead to Bridal Veil Falls

The hike to the top of Bridal Veil Falls starts at a large parking area just past the Pandora Mill at the east end of Telluride (see the driving directions below). From the parking area follow the dirt and gravel jeep road as it switchbacks up the northeast wall of the dramatic box canyon at the head of the Telluride valley. Colorful eroded canyon walls loom overhead while in the distance Bridal Veil Falls, Colorado's tallest free falling waterfall, plunges 365-ft. from just beneath the Bridal Veil power plant.

After negotiating a few switchbacks the road straightens out for about 0.5 miles, continuing its steady ascent to the canyon's headwall. At the headwall the road climbs a series of long sweeping switchbacks to a dramatic viewpoint at the base of the falls. The viewpoint, located 1.2 miles from the start at a hairpin curve on one of the switchbacks, is often enveloped in mist from the water thundering over the rock face and hitting a small pool at the base of the falls.

The remaining 0.8 miles of the hike to the top of the falls enjoys wonderful views of Telluride Valley. Along the way great views open to the power plant perched on a ledge just above the falls. The building, restored in the 1990's, is listed on the National Register of Historic places.

The power plant, the second oldest AC generation facility in the country, was built in 1907 to supply the Smuggler's Union Mine. Water driving the generators is piped from Blue Lake (see Blue Lake trail description).

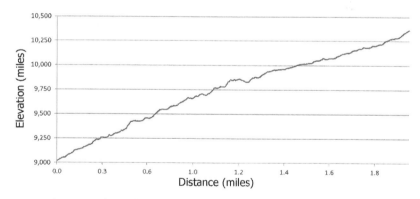

At the top of the fourth switchback from the base of the falls you will see a gate blocking vehicle access to the power plant. This is the beginning of the hiking trail up Bridal Veil basin. (The jeep road takes a sharp left before the gate, continuing its climb to Ingram Basin on the notorious Black Bear 4WD road.)

Duck through the large openings in the gate and follow the old mining road for a short distance to a view point just above the power plant (on your right). Please stay on the road. The building and the area around the plant is private property.

While this is the turnaround point for many people, the pretty basin encourages further exploration. For more information on walks in the basin see the Blue Lake and Lewis Lake and Mine trail descriptions.

Note that two-way traffic is permitted on the jeep road between the Pandora Mine and the Power plant. The Black Bear Road above the power plant is one way – heading downhill toward Telluride. (The Black Bear Road starts south of Red Mountain Pass on Highway 550, goes over Black Bear Pass (12,840-ft.) and descends Ingram Basin on dangerous and difficult switchbacks to meet the jeep road coming up from Telluride.)

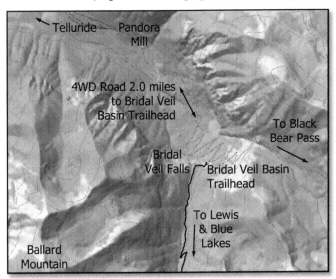

My advice is to get an early start if you plan to do this walk. Jeep traffic is much lighter in the morning due to the one-way restrictions on the Black Bear road. The road is also a favorite of mountain bikers. Keep a watch at all times for mountain bikes flying down the road.

Driving Directions

From Telluride: Drive east through Telluride on Colorado Avenue for a little over 2.0 miles past the Pandora Mill to a large unmarked parking area and park.

19. See Forever / Bear Creek Loop ★★★★☆

Distance: 5.5 - 8.4 miles (loop)

This interesting loop hike features panoramic views of Telluride, Bear Creek Canyon and the distant peaks of the Lizard Head Wilderness.

Distance: 5.5 miles (RT) to See Forever
1.5 miles (one-way) See Forever to Wasatch via Connector Trail
8.4 miles (loop) to Telluride via the Wasatch and Bear Creek Trails
Elevation: 10,540-ft. at Trailhead
12,100-ft. at See Forever
11,530-ft. at end of the Wasatch Connector Trail
8,820 at Telluride (end of the Wasatch/Bear Creek Trail
Elevation Gain: 1,560-ft. to See Forever
-570-ft. at the end of the Wasatch Connector Trail
-2,710-ft. (loss) to Telluride via the Wasatch/Bear Creek Trails

Difficulty: strenuous
Basecamp: Telluride
Area: Uncompahgre NF
Best Season: July - September
USGS Map(s): Telluride

Why Hike the See Forever / Bear Creek Loop

This interesting loop hike, starting at the St. Sophia gondola station in the Telluride Ski Area, is actually a combination of four trails, the See Forever, the Wasatch Connector, a segment of the Wasatch trail and the Bear Creek trail, each with its own distinct personality.

Be forewarned that the See Forever portion of the hike traverses ski slopes and follows gravel ski service roads. While I am typically not a big fan of road walking or hiking in ski areas the panoramic views of peaks rising above the Telluride Valley and the Lizard Head Wilderness more than compensate for the less than desirable trail conditions for the first 2.75 miles of the hike to the Wasatch Connector trail.

Just 0.4 miles down the Wasatch Connector trail you leave the ski area behind and head for the beautiful upper basin of the Bear Creek drainage and dramatic Bear Creek Canyon. This portion of the trail enjoys wonderful views of the Wasatch basin, the incredible peaks defining the north wall of the Telluride Valley and the sculpted cliffs of the Bear Creek canyon.

Note that the 8.4-mile loop is best done in a counter-clockwise direction and involves sections of steep switchbacks gaining 1,540-ft. and dropping 3,280-ft. (Reverse the gains and losses if you hike in a clockwise direction.)

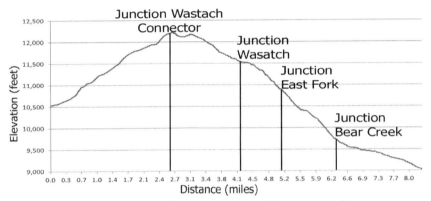

Trailhead to the junction with the Wasatch Connector Trail

Distance from Trailhead: 5.5 miles (RT)
Elevation: 12,100-ft.
Elevation Gain: 1,560-ft.

While the trail can be hiked in either direction, I recommend starting at the St. Sophia gondola station at 10,540-ft. and hiking in a counter-clockwise direction (see driving directions below). This starting point limits the elevation gain to 1,540-ft. versus the alternative start at Bear Creek that involves a 3,280-ft gain.

Telluride's free gondola links the town of Telluride with the Mountain Village, located south of town behind the San Sophia ridge. The St. Sophia station is an intermediate stop on the gondola, providing access to hiking, biking and ski trails.

Exit the gondola station and walk south for 0.4-miles, following a gravel ski access road uphill to a snowmaking pond. The start of the See Forever trail is marked by a Forest Service sign on the left side of the road just past the south end of the pond.

The trail traverses a tree covered hillside to the See Forever ski run, where a series of steep steps climb the western side of the run to a junction with the Lookout ski trail that heads downhill to Telluride. While climbing the steps enjoy wonderful views of the peaks and ridges rising to the north and northeast of Telluride. To the west are distance views of the San Miguel Mountains and the Lizard Head Wilderness.

At the junction the hiking trail crosses to the eastern side of the ski slope where a sign with a photograph identifies the peaks to the north/northeast. After taking in the view follow the trail, now on the eastern side of the See Forever run, as it continues its steep ascent.

About 1.2 miles from the Gondola station signs for the See Forever hiking trail direct you to follow a gravel ski road, which switchbacks steeply up the ridge. The views of Lizard Head and the peaks to the north of Telluride help you ignore that you are walking through a ski area on a road.

At 1.8 miles the grade abates a bit. Be sure to watch for the trail signs directing you to stay right at the intersection of two ski roads. (The road to the left heads to the top of a ski lift). A short distance beyond the intersection views open to the east (your left) to the cliffs lining the eastern wall of Bear Creek canyon.

Continue following the road as it climbs the ridge to meet the Wasatch Connector trail, which branches left from the road at 2.75 miles. At this point it is worth following the ski road for a short distance to a crest on the ridge. This section of the trail enjoys wonderful 360-degree views of the surrounding area. The 14,000-ft. peaks of the Lizard Head Wilderness dominate the skyline to the west. To the north the peaks and ridges of the Sneffels range tower above Telluride, to the east are the sculpted and highly eroded walls of the Bear Creek drainage while to the southeast Wasatch Mountain and the San Joaquin Ridge rise above the East Fork of the Bear Creek basin. Directly to the south a steep road climbs over 300-ft in 0.3-miles to the top of Gold Hill.

Wasatch Connector Trail to the junction with the Wasatch Trail

Segment Distance: 1.5 miles (one-way)
Ending Elevation: 11,530-ft.
Elevation Gain/Loss: -570-ft.

If you wish to do the loop hike after soaking in the scenery head back to the Wasatch Connector and follow the trail as it traverses the Revelation ski bowl below Gold Hill. At 3.1 miles the trail crosses a minor ridge, leaving the ski area behind, and starts a steep descent on a rocky trail that loses 570 feet in a little over a mile. Views of Bear Creek canyon, the East Fork/Wasatch basin and the Telluride valley make it hard to keep your eyes on the narrow trail.

The connector trail ends at Bear Creek and the Wasatch Trail at 4.2 miles, where a sign points back to the ski area and across the basin to the upper portion of the Wasatch trail, which crosses the creek and ascends a grassy hillside on the other side of the drainage.

Wasatch and Bear Creek Trails back to Telluride

Segment Stats: 4.2 miles (one-way) with a 2,710-ft. elevation loss
Loop Distance: 8.4 miles (loop)
Maximum Elevation: 11,530-ft. to 8,820 feet at the trailhead in Telluride
Elevation Gain/Loss for the Loop: 1,560-ft. / -3.280-ft.

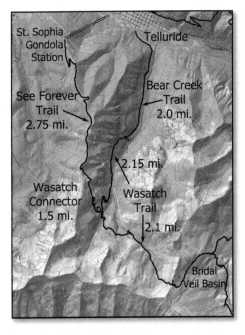

Look for a sign that simply says "trail" pointing to north (downhill) on the western side of the creek. This is the section of the Wasatch trail we will descend to meet the Bear Creek trail, which will take us back to Telluride.

At the trail junction Bear Creek drops steeply down a rocky gorge. To circumvent the gorge, the narrow Wasatch trail contours north along the hillside, staying high above the creek for 0.75 miles, then drops steeply down to the creek on switchbacks, losing 500-ft. in about 0.5 miles. The trail meets the creek just above the junction with the East Fork Bear Creek trail. (The East Fork Bear Creek trail climbs the eastern side of the East Fork to meet the Wasatch trail in 0.9 miles in the upper East Fork/Wasatch basin.)

Continue following the Wasatch trail downhill. In a short distance you will pass the remnants of the Nellie mine on your left. Beyond the mine the trail descends a steep gully, then traverses the western canyon wall high above the creek. This scenic section of the trail offers great views of the cliffs towering above the canyon.

The final leg of the Wasatch trail drops steeply on switchbacks through groves of aspen and mixed conifers to the junction with the Bear Creek trail at 6.4 miles. While descending the final set of switchbacks look up canyon for nice views of beautiful Bear Creek Falls. (A 0.6 miles round-trip detour leads from the trail junction to a viewpoint near the base of the falls.)

The rest of the 2.0-mile walk is a breeze, following a wide dirt track descending the western side of the Bear Creek drainage back to Telluride at 8.4 miles. See the Bear Creek trail description for more information.

Note: The loop hike loses 3,280-ft. in elevation from the start of the Wasatch Connector trail at 12,100-ft. to the beginning of the Bear Creek trail at 8,820-ft.

Driving Directions

To the St. Sophia Gondola Station in Telluride: In Telluride, CO, walk to the gondola located on San Juan Avenue, 3 blocks south of the main street (Colorado Avenue). Take the free gondola to the top of the mountain, exiting at the St. Sophia station. From the gondola station, walk south on the Nature Trail for about 200 yards to the log cabin. Continue on the adjacent road (Basin Road/Trail) for approximately 300 yards as it proceeds south past the Village Trailhead sign to the snowmaking pond and See Forever Trailhead sign on the left.

To the Bear Creek Trailhead in Telluride: From Telluride's main street (Colorado Avenue), turn south onto Pine Street, proceed several blocks, continuing as the street turns into a dirt road that becomes the Bear Creek Trail.

Note: Parking in Telluride can be difficult. Parking is by permit only on many of the streets in the residential section of town and is limited to two-hour parking along Colorado Avenue and its adjacent side streets. Free day-use parking is available in Carhenge Lot, just off West Pacific Avenue at the west end of town near the base of Lift 7, or at the south end of Mahoney Drive, near the west entrance to town. A free shuttle bus, called the Galloping Goose, runs between the parking lots and various stops in downtown Telluride.

There is also free parking in the mountain village. From there you can take the free gondola to/from the St. Sophia Gondola Station and town.

20. Wasatch Trail ★★★★★
Distance: 12.3 miles (RT)

Dramatic views of Bear Creek Canyon, beautiful alpine basins, wildflowers and waterfalls are a few of the delights on this steep trail to visit the saddle (13,050-ft.) on the divide between Bear Creek and Bridal Veil basins. The hike includes an initial 2.0-mile segment of the popular Bear Creek Falls trail.

Distance: 12.3 miles (RT)	**Basecamp:** Telluride
Elevation: 8,800-ft. at Trailhead	**Area:** Uncompahgre NF
13,050-ft. at Wasatch Saddle	**Best Season:** July - September
Elevation Gain: 4,250-ft.	**USGS Map(s):** Telluride
Difficulty: strenuous	**See Page 94 for Map**

Why Hike the Wasatch Trail

Many people hike beautiful Bear Creek Canyon to the waterfall. Fewer continue beyond, up the canyon on the Wasatch trail.

The steep hike to the upper canyon and into the Wasatch Basin is well worth the effort. In the upper canyon hikers are rewarded with dramatic views of the sculpted and highly eroded walls of the Bear Creek drainage. Beyond the canyon the Wasatch trail traverses beautiful flower-filled alpine meadows nestled in a narrow cirque beneath Wasatch Mountain and the San Joaquin Ridge before climbing to a 13,050-ft. divide separating the Bear Creek and Bridal Veil Basins.

It is possible to make a long loop out of the hike by crossing the saddle and returning via Bridal Veil Basin. Walking the entire loop, including the road down from the Bridal Veil Power Plant and back to downtown Telluride, is about 14.3 miles. The better option is to get dropped at the Bridal Veil Power plant and do the hike in reverse, up Bridal Veil basin and down the Wasatch. This reduces the elevation gain to 2,650-ft. from 4,250-ft. and cuts 4.0-miles off the trip. (See the hike to Lewis Lake and Mine for more information on the hike up Bridal Veil basin.)

Bear Creek Trailhead to the junction with the Wasatch Connector

Distance from Trailhead: 8.2 miles (RT)
Elevation: 11,530-ft.
Elevation Gain: 2,730-ft.

Follow the Bear Creek trail, a wide dirt track shared with bikers and horseback riders, as it climbs at a steady pace through a forest of aspen and mixed conifers. As you ascend the trees thin and intermittent meadows provide fine views of the dramatic cliffs defining the canyon's eastern wall.

Reach the junction with the Wasatch trail after walking 2.0-miles and gaining 1,380-ft. Turn right (west) at the junction on the Wasatch Trail and follow the narrow path as it climbs steeply on switchbacks through groves of aspen and evergreens, gaining 575-ft. in over 0.5 miles. At the top of the switchbacks the grade abates and the trail traverses high above the canyon floor for about a mile, eventually meeting Bear Creek at the base of a gully.

Ascend the gully on a steep track. Bear Creek cascades over rocks and wood debris in the stream bed next to the trail. Near the top of the gully pass the remnants of the Nellie mine on the right (west) side of the trail.

Beyond the mine cross a debris pile caused by a rock slide and come to junction with the East Fork Bear Creek trail. The East Fork Bear Creek trail, going left at the junction, climbs the eastern side of the East Fork of Bear Creek for 0.9 miles to meet the Wasatch trail in the upper East Fork basin. This section is much shorter but also considerably steeper than the alternative route up the Wasatch trail. Some hikers make a loop out of the

Wasatch and East Fork or simply use it as an alternate means of descending from the Wasatch Basin on the return hike.

My advice is to go right at the trail junction and stay on the Wasatch. To circumvent the basin's rocky headwall, the trail climbs a steep series of switchbacks, gaining 500-ft. in 0.5 miles, and then traverses the canyon's western wall on a gentle grade to meet Bear Creek at the top of the headwall. A short distance from the top of the headwall the Wasatch meets the Wasatch Connector trail descending from the ski area to the west (right).

Wasatch Connector Junction to the Saddle

Segment Stat: 2.1 miles (one-way) with a 1,520-ft. elevation gain
Distance - Trailhead to the Saddle: 12.3 miles (RT)
Elevation at the Saddle: 13,050-ft.
Elevation Gain - Trailhead to the Saddle: 4,250-ft.

At the signed junction turn left (east) and follow the Wasatch Trail as it crossed Bear Creek and then climbs steeply through meadows to a shelf atop a rocky knoll. As you climb enjoy the fine views extending north/northwest across the Telluride Valley and west to the Gold Hill ski area.

At the top of the knoll the trail drops gently to and crosses the East Fork of Bear Creek, arriving at a junction where the East Fork of Bear Creek trail rejoins the Wasatch. Go right (east) at the junction and follow the trail as it ascends 600-ft. over a mile through wildflower-filled meadows toward the base of the saddle at the head of the cirque anchored by the San Joaquin Ridge to the south and Wasatch Mountain (13,555-ft.) to the north.

The final ascent to the saddle is quite steep, climbing almost 500-ft in just under 0.5 miles. From the saddle views extend west toward the San Joaquin Ridge and Silver Mountain. To the east are the peaks and ridge rising above upper Bridal Veil Basin.

Once you are done soaking in the scenery, turn around and retrace your steps. For variety you can take the East Fork trail on the return leg, but be forewarned that it is quite steep.

With planning it is possible to extend the hike into a long loop by crossing the saddle and returning via Bridal Veil Basin. Walking the entire loop, including the road down from the Bridal Veil Power Plant to the Pandora Mine and back to downtown Telluride, is close to 14.3 miles. The better option is to get dropped at the Bridal Veil Power plant and do the hike in reverse, up Bridal Veil basin and down the Wasatch. This reduces the elevation gain to 2,650-ft. from 4,250-ft. and cuts 4.0-miles off the trip.

To do the loop, descend the east side of the saddle to a unmarked junction. Turn left (northeast) and descend through Bridal Veil Basin. (The trail to the right climbs to saddle and ends up in Ophir.) At the first intersection, marked by a post, head left (northeast). The trail to the right climbs to Lewis Lake and Mine.

Follow the trail, which starts as a double track and then becomes a gravel road, down the basin to the Bridal Veil Power Plant, where hopefully a car awaits to take you back to Telluride. If not, walk down the Bridal Veil 4WD road to the Pandora Mine and then follow the Idarado Legacy Trail and the San Miguel River Trail back to town. Note the walk from the power plant to town is 4.0-miles.

See the Lewis Lake and Mine trail description for more information on hiking Bridal Veil basin.

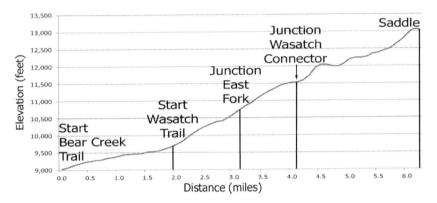

Driving Directions

From Telluride: From Telluride's main street (Colorado Avenue), turn south onto Pine Street, proceed several blocks, continuing as the street turns into a dirt road that becomes the Bear Creek Trail. Proceed south on the trail for 2.0 miles to the Wasatch Trail.

Note: Parking in Telluride can be difficult. Parking is by permit only on many of the streets in the residential section of town and is limited to two-hour parking along Colorado Avenue and its adjacent side streets. Free day-use parking is available in Carhenge Lot, just off West Pacific Avenue at the west end of town near the base of Lift 7, or at the south end of Mahoney Drive, near the west entrance to town. A free shuttle bus, called the Galloping Goose, runs between the parking lots and various stops in downtown Telluride.

There is also free parking in the mountain village. From there you can take the free gondola to town and walk to the trailhead.

21. Bear Creek Falls ★★★★★

Distance: 4.6 miles (RT)

This half day hike up Bear Creek Canyon offers scenic views of the rugged cliffs lining the canyon and ends at a pretty waterfall. It's a nice option if you have limited time or just want an easy day.

Distance: 4.6 miles (RT)
Elevation: 8,800-ft. at Trailhead
9,940-ft. at Bear Creek Falls
Elevation Gain: 1,140-ft.
Difficulty: easy-moderate

Basecamp: Telluride
Area: Uncompahgre NF
Best Season: July - September
USGS Map(s): Telluride
See Page 94 for Map

Why Hike Blue Lake Falls

A pretty waterfall and scenic views of the rugged cliffs lining Bear Creek canyon is your reward for hiking 2.3 miles up the Bear Creek trail from Telluride. The popular trail, which is shared with bikers and horseback riders, is a good workout and great way to acclimate. The trail connects with the Wasatch trail that heads further up the canyon and provides options for longer loop hikes to Telluride's ski area and Bridal Veil basin.

Trailhead to Bear Creek Falls

The Bear Creek trail starts on the end of South Pine Street (see driving directions) on a wide dirt track shared with bikers and horseback riders. Follow the trail as it heads up hill to a sign marking the beginning of the Bear Creek Preserve. The San Miguel Conservation Foundation, in partnership with the town of Telluride, acquired and donated a 320-acre parcel of land in the Bear Creek Canyon to the citizens of Telluride in 1995 to preserve Bear Creek as public open space.

Beyond the sign the trail heads southeast toward Bear Creek Canyon, climbing through a forest of aspen and mixed conifers. Openings in the trees offer nice views to the north of the cliffs and peaks towering above Telluride.

At 0.6 miles the trail swings to the south and enters the canyon, continuing its ascent along the west side of Bear Creek, which can't be seen from the trail. After hiking about 1.2 miles the trees start to thin and meadows appear along the trail. From the meadows and opening in the trees enjoy great views of the dramatic cliffs defining the canyon's eastern wall.

The scenery continues to improve as you climb. At just under 1.7 miles the creek comes into view at a pretty spot with a small waterfall. Rock cairns of all shapes and sizes decorate the meadow by the creek.

Reach a junction with the Wasatch trail in a large open meadow at 2.0 miles. Beautiful Bear Creek Falls is seen through the trees cascading down a rocky cliff at the head of a small basin. Continue straight ahead on trail for 0.3 miles, following the path as it wandering beside the creek through meadows to the base of the falls. (The Wasatch trail branches to the right (west) and climbs the hillside above the trail.)

After exploring the falls, retrace your steps, enjoying nice views of the peaks and ridgelines rising to the north of Telluride.

Hikers with the time and energy will want to explore further up canyon on the Wasatch trail. The Bear Creek trail is also used as part of a loop that connects with the See Forever trail. (See the Wasatch trail and See Forever trail descriptions for more information.)

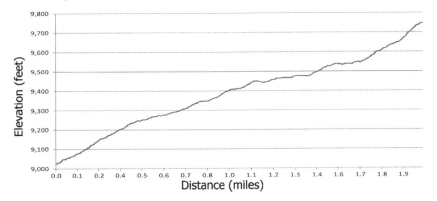

Driving Directions

From Telluride: From Telluride's main street (Colorado Avenue), turn south onto Pine Street, proceed several blocks, continuing as the street turns into a dirt road that becomes the Bear Creek Trail.

Note: Parking in Telluride can be difficult. Parking is by permit only on many of the streets in the residential section of town and is limited to two-hour parking along Colorado Avenue and its adjacent side streets. Free day-use parking is available in Carhenge Lot, just off West Pacific Avenue at the west end of town near the base of Lift 7, or at the south end of Mahoney Drive, near the west entrance to town. A free shuttle bus, called the Galloping Goose, runs between the parking lots and various stops in downtown Telluride.

There is also free parking in the mountain village. From there you can take the free gondola to town and walk to the trailhead.

22. Lake Hope ★★★★★
Distance: 4.5 - 5.9 miles (RT)

This popular hike to a high alpine lake surround by 13,000-ft. peaks offers panoramic views of the Wilson Range and the high peaks in the Lizard Head Wilderness along the way.

Distance: 4.5 miles (RT) to Lake
5.9 miles (RT) to Unnamed Pass
Elevation: 10,750-ft. at Trailhead
11,880-ft. at Lake Hope
12,445-ft. at Unnamed Pass
Elevation Gain: 1,130-ft. to Lake
1,695-ft. to Unnamed Pass

Difficulty: moderate
Basecamp: Telluride
Area: Uncompahgre NF
Best Season: July - September
USGS Map(s): Ophir

Why Hike to Lake Hope

The red, rust and purplish-gray colors of Vermilion Peak form the backdrop for brilliant green meadows filled with a spectacular display of wildflowers. In the distance the fourteeners of the Wilson Range and the distinctive spire of Lizard Head Peak fills the western skyline. These views and others, both near and far, are the reason to hike to Lake Hope and the unnamed pass above this pretty glacial lake.

This moderately-easy hike is deservedly popular, so you won't be alone. Get an early start and pick a weekday to avoid the crowds. You won't be sorry.

Trailhead to Lake Hope

Distance from Trailhead: 4.5 miles (RT)
Elevation at Lake Hope: 11,880-ft.
Elevation Gain: 1,130-ft.

The Lake Hope trail, which starts at a sharp curve on a switchback on FS Road #627 (see driving directions below), ascends through spruce-fir forest on gentle grades up the east side of the Lake Fork valley. A stream crossing at Poverty Gulch (0.3 miles) provides the first views of Sheep Mountain and San Miguel Peak (13,752-ft.) across the valley.

Continuing up valley the path crosses rock slides and traverses small wildflower-filled meadows that offer sweeping views of the fourteeners of the Wilson Range and the distinctive spire of Lizard Head Peak to the northwest. As you climb enjoy ever improving views of the peaks lining the south and west walls of the valley. To the east above to the trail a large rust-colored scree field spills off the shoulder of Vermilion Peak.

At the head of the valley the trail swings southwest through meadows filled with waist-high wildflowers. After crossing the third stream, about 45 minutes from the start of the hike, the trail begins a moderate-steep climb, aided by switchbacks, through woods up the headwall of the lake basin. Openings in the trees provide nice views of Trout Lake and nearby peaks.

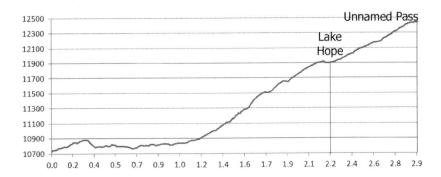

After gaining 800-ft. in 0.6 miles the trees give way to beautiful meadows sprinkled with wildflowers. To your left (east) the skyline is dominated by Vermilion Peak, clad in red, rust and purple-gray rock, rising above the emerald green alpine basin.

Lake Hope (11,880-ft.), at 2.25 miles, comes as somewhat of a surprise, springing into view as you crest a grassy slope between two rocky hills. The man-made lake, storing water for the Ames Power Plant, sits in a pretty cirque surrounded on three sides by 13,000-ft. peaks. Use trails extend along the lake's eastern shore to a dam at the north end of the lake.

Lake Hope to Unnamed Pass

Segment Stat: 0.7 miles (one-way) with a 565-ft. elevation gain
Distance - Trailhead to the Pass: 5.9 miles (RT)
Elevation at the Pass: 12,445-ft.
Elevation Gain - Trailhead to the Pass: 1,695-ft.

The trail to the pass above Lake Hope heads south around the east (left) side of the lake and soon starts climbing a moderately steep slope through meadows dotted with wildflowers. At 2.6 miles the trail swings east and switchbacks up a rocky hillside, reaching the unnamed pass in 0.7 miles after gaining 545-ft.

From the pass enjoy views of Rolling Mountain (13,693) to the south and the Twin Sisters (13,374 and 13,432) to the east. San Miguel Peak dominates the scenic ridge rising above Lake Hope to the west.

After taking a break return the way you came, enjoying the great views as you descend. Allow 4 to 4.5 hours for the round trip hike to the pass, including a lunch break.

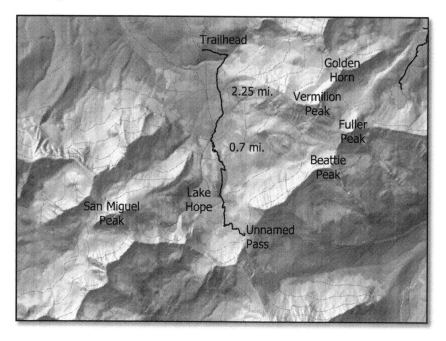

Driving Directions

From Telluride: From downtown Telluride drive 3 miles west on West Colorado Avenue (the main street) to the intersection with State Hwy 145 and turn left (south). Follow Hwy 145 for approximately 10.1 miles and take a left at the road signed for Trout Lake (Forest Road #626/ North Trout Lake Road). Follow the road around the northwest shore of Trout lake for approximately one mile to Forest Road #627. Turn left on #627. Proceed up this rough road for 2.5 miles to the Hope Lake Trailhead. The trailhead is located on the sharp curve of a switchback. (Note: High clearance vehicles are recommended for FS627. Passenger cars, driven carefully, have successfully negotiated the road. It is best to check with the Forest Service to learn about current road conditions.)

23. Lizard Head ★★★★★
Distance: 7.6 - 11.7 miles (loop)

One of the top hikes in the Telluride area, this scenic loop traverses the panoramic spine of Blackface Mountain on its way to the base of Lizard Head Peak (13,113-ft.), an eroded 400-ft. tall spire shaped like the gaping maw of a lizard with its face to the sky.

Distance: 7.6 miles (RT) to Black Face Peak
11.7 miles (loop) on Loop via Cross Mountain and old Railroad Grade
Elevation: 10,250-ft. at Trailhead
12,147-ft. at Black Face Peak
Elevation Gain: 1,897-ft. to Black Face Peak
2,900-ft. on Loop via Cross Mountain and old Railroad Grade
Difficulty: strenuous

Basecamp: Telluride
Area: Lizard Head Wilderness, San Juan and Uncompahgre NF
Best Season: July - September
USGS Map(s): Mt. Wilson

Why Hike Lizard Head

The Lizard Head trail traversing Black Face Mountain's broad, panoramic ridge is not the shortest route to the base of Lizard Head peak but it is certainly the most scenic. From the ridge leading to the top of Black Face Mountain, the San Miguel Range, including Mount Wilson (14,245-ft.), Gladstone Mountain (13,913-ft.) and Wilson Peak (14,017-ft.), forms a dramatic backdrop for Lizard Head's lone spire soaring 400-ft. above its rocky pedestal.

To the east spectacular views encompass Trout Lake and the peaks surrounding the Lake Hope basin, including Sheep Mountain, Pilot Knob, Golden Horn and Vermillion Peak. To the north, Sunshine Mountain rises above picturesque Wilson Meadows. In the distance, to the northeast, is the jagged profile of the Mt. Sneffels range.

The trail can either be done as an out-and-back hike or a loop using the Cross Mountain and the old Railroad Grade route on the return leg. The loop covers 11.7 miles of diverse terrain with a net elevation gain over 2,900-ft.

Be aware the loop hike follows ridges and crosses high alpine meadows for over 4 miles. These areas are dangerous places to be in the event of a thunderstorm. Pick a nice day and get an early start so that you are down from the high country before the onset of afternoon thunder storms, a frequent occurrence on summer afternoons in the Rockies.

Trailhead to Black Face Peak

Distance from Trailhead: 7.6 miles (RT)
Elevation: 12,147-ft.
Elevation Gain: 1,897-ft.

The Lizard Head trail heads northeast from the parking area (see driving directions below) on easy grades through pretty meadows and forests of aspen and mixed conifers beneath the steep south face of Black Face Mountain (12,147-ft.). Openings in the trees provide views of Trout Lake and the jagged ridge of 13,000-ft.-plus peaks rising to the east.

After 1.5 miles the trail swings left (west) and starts a moderately steep ascent on switchbacks through spruce-fir forest and meadows, at times skirting the edge of talus slopes, to a junction with the Wilson Meadows trail (heading straight ahead). Keep left, staying on the Lizard Head trail as it climbs steeply up switchbacks on a forested slope. As you climb, the trees gives way to rocky slopes. Reach the ridge leading to the summit of Black Face at 3.0 miles after gaining 1,400-ft.

As the trail attains the ridge top the rocky slopes give way to alpine meadows dotted with wildflowers. Watch for posts to help guide you through areas where the trail is indistinct.

The path now ascends on gentle to moderate grades along the ridge to the summit of Black Face (12,147-ft.) at 3.8 miles. Along the way enjoy spectacular views to the east of Trout Lake and the peaks surrounding the Lake Hope basin, including Sheep Mountain, Pilot Knob, Golden Horn and

Vermillion Peak. To the west the skyline is dominated by Lizard Head's distinctive profile set against a backdrop of the high peaks of the San Miguel range, including Mount Wilson (14,245-ft.), Gladstone Mountain (13,913-ft.) and Wilson Peak (14,017-ft.). Sunshine Mountain (12,930-ft.) towers above the beautiful emerald green expanse of Wilson Meadows to the north. In the distance to the northeast is the jagged profile of the Sneffels range.

The summit of Black Face Mountain is a good turn around point for hikers looking for a shorter day or if the weather is taking a turn for the worse.

Black Face to Junction with the Cross Mountain Trail

Segment Stat: 2.3 miles with a 780-ft. elevation loss and 600-ft. elevation gain.
Distance - Trailhead to the Cross Mountain: 6.3 miles (one-way)
Ending Elevation: 12,080-ft.
Elevation Gain/Loss - Trailhead to Cross Mountain: 2,497-ft. / -780-ft.

To continue the loop follow the trail down the west side of the ridge to a saddle between the Wilson Creek and Lizard Head drainages, losing about 630-ft. From the saddle the trail ascends a rocky slope on moderate grades and then swings southwest, traversing high meadows to cross a ridge (12,080-ft.) jutting from Lizard Head's southern flank at 5.9 miles. From the saddle to the ridge the trail gains about 600-ft.

Hikers continuing along this segment of the trail are rewarded with amazing views of Lizard Head towering above the trail. The 13,113-ft. eroded volcanic plug was called, "one of the most difficult of Colorado's summits to reach," by Robert Ormes in his 1979 Guide to Colorado Mountains.

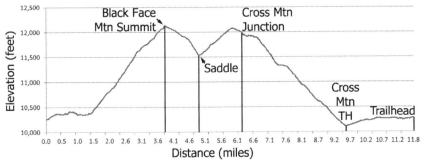

Anyone except the experienced parties thinking about scaling the peak should heed Ormes' warning, "our advice when you reach the base, take [a] picture and go home."

Take a break at the top of the ridge to enjoy the spectacular views of the high peaks of the San Miguel range. From the ridge top the trail loses about 150-ft. as it contours beneath Lizard Head to the junction with the Cross Mountain trail at 6.25-miles.

Optional Bilk Basin Overlook extension

Distance from the Cross Mountain junction: 0.6 miles (RT)
Elevation of the Bilk Basin Overlook: 12,114-ft.
Elevation Gain to the Bilk Basin Overlook from the Junction: 180-ft.

A quick side trip to the Bilk Basin overlook is highly recommended if you have the time and energy. To reach the overlook from the Cross Mountain junction, continue along the Lizard Head trail as it ascends northwest through rocky meadows to a saddle, 0.3 miles from the junction. This wonderful vantage point features panoramic views of Bilk Basin and the jagged peaks and ridges of the San Miguel Range, including Mount Wilson, Gladstone Peak and Wilson Peak, towering above the west side of the basin. After soaking in the views, return to the Cross Mountain trail junction (11,940-ft.).

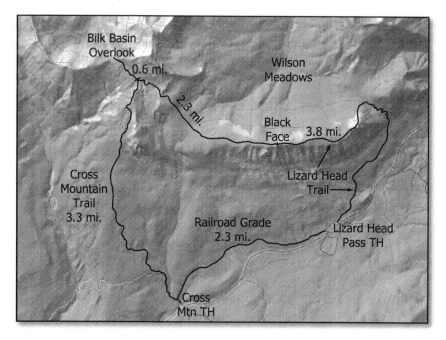

Cross Mountain and old Railroad Grade to Lizard Head Trailhead

Segment Stat: 5.6 miles from the junction of the Cross Mountain trail back to the Lizard Head trailhead using the Cross Mountain and old Railroad Grade trails.
Total Distance for the Loop Hike: 11.7 miles (loop)
Maximum Elevation: 11,940-ft.
Elevation Gain/Loss for the Loop: 2,900-ft. / -2,900-ft.

To complete the 11.7-mile loop, using the Cross Mountain trail and the old Railroad Grade back to the Lizard Head Parking lot, head downhill on the Cross Mountain trail. The trail descends through meadows and spruce/fir forest, losing 1,900-ft in 3.25 miles as it drops to a parking area just off Highway 145. (For more information see the Cross Mountain trail description.)

Just before reaching the highway you will see a wide, unmarked trail/dirt road heading left (northeast) through open meadows. The wide path ascends on easy grades along an old railroad grade that essentially parallels Highway 145 for 2.25 miles back to the Lizard Head Pass parking area. (See the Railroad Grade route description for more information.)

Driving Directions

From Telluride: Drive south from Telluride on Colorado 145 for 12.3 miles to Lizard Head Pass. On the right (west) side of the highway is a rest area and interpretive site. Turn right into the rest area and park. The trailhead is located at the northeast end of the parking area. You can also park in a separate trailhead parking area by driving through the rest area (past the restroom) for approximately 1000-ft., then turn right onto a spur road that ends at the Lizard Head trailhead parking area.

24. Cross Mountain ★★★★★
Distance: 6.6 miles (RT)

A nice hike to the base of Lizard Head Peak, a distinctive 13,113-ft. rock spire towering above Highway 145 just south of Lizard Head Pass.

Distance: 6.6 miles (RT)
Elevation: 10,040-ft. at Trailhead
11,940-ft. at Cross Mountain
Elevation Gain: 1,900-ft.
Difficulty: moderate-strenuous

Basecamp: Telluride
Area: Lizard Head Wilderness, Uncompahgre NF
Best Season: July - September
USGS Map(s): Mt. Wilson
See Page 107 for Map

Why Hike Cross Mountain

There are two main routes to the base of Lizard Head Peak (13,113-ft.), the landmark 400-ft. tall pinnacle in the Lizard Head Wilderness. Cross Mountain is the shorter more direct, albeit less scenic, route when compared to the Lizard Head Trail.

The trail can either be done as an out-and-back hike or a loop combining the Lizard Head and the Railroad Grade trails on the return leg. The loop covers 11.7 miles of diverse terrain with a net elevation gain of over 2,700-ft.

Be aware the loop hike follows ridges and crosses high alpine meadows for over 4 miles. These areas are dangerous places to be in the event of a thunderstorm. Pick and nice day and get an early start so that you are down from the high country before the onset of afternoon thunder storms, a frequent occurrence on summer afternoons in the Rockies.

Trailhead to Junction with the Lizard Head Trail

Distance from Trailhead: 6.6 miles (RT)
Elevation: 11,940-ft.
Elevation Gain: 1,900-ft.

From the parking area the trail crosses a creek on a bridge and heads northwest, crossing a dirt track along the way. For the first half mile the Cross Mountain trail ascends through meadows with views to the east of the peaks and ridges around the Trout Lake area, including Sheep Mountain, Vermilion Peak, Golden Horn and Pilot Knob. At the 0.4-mile mark pass the junction with the Groundhog Stock trail (heading left). Shortly after the junction the trail enters a spruce-fir forest with restricted views.

After 1.9 miles and an elevation gain of 1,200-ft., the trees give way to open meadows with ever improving views. Soon Lizard Head Peak comes into view along with the high peaks of the San Miguel Range, including Cross Mountain, Mt. Wilson and Gladstone Peak.

After climbing 1,900-ft. in 3.25 miles the trail arrives at the junction with the Lizard Head trail at the base of Lizard Head Peak, a distinctive 400-ft. rock spire. The 13,113-ft. peak, an old, eroded volcanic plug looming above the trail, is said to look like the gaping maw of a lizard with its face to the sky. From this vantage point it is hard to see the likeness.

Resist any temptation to climb the spire. Robert Ormes, publisher of one of the first guidebooks to the Colorado Mountains, issued the following warning about climbing the peak in his 1979 edition of the Guide to the Colorado Mountains:

"Lizard Head is the most difficult of Colorado summits to reach. In fact the rottenness of its 400-ft. tower makes safety too much a matter of luck for comfort. Returning visitors have formed the opinion that the peak has become noticeably rottener and more dangerous. Our advice when you reach the base, take [a] picture and go home."

After admiring the pinnacle many people will turn around and return to the trailhead.

Optional Bilk Basin Overlook Extension

Distance from Junction to Bilk Basin Overlook: 0.6 miles (RT)
Elevation at Bilk Basin Overlook: 12,114-ft.
Elevation Gain from Junction to Bilk Basin Overlook: 180-ft.

A quick side trip to the Bilk Basin overlook is highly recommended if you have the time and energy. To reach the overlook, turn left at the junction and follow the Lizard Head trail as it ascends northwest through rocky meadows to a saddle, 0.3 miles from the junction. This wonderful vantage point features panoramic views of Bilk Basin and the jagged peaks and ridges of the San Miguel Range, including Mount Wilson, Gladstone Peak and Wilson Peak, towering above the west side of the basin. After soaking in the views, return to the Cross Mountain trail junction.

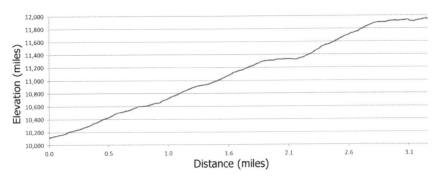

Lizard Head and old Railroad Grade to Cross Mountain Trailhead

Segment Stats: 8.4 miles (one-way) with a 780-ft. elevation gain and 2,700-ft. elevation loss
Distance: 11.7 miles (loop)
Maximum Elevation: 12,147-ft.
Elevation Gain/Loss for the Loop: 2,900-ft. / -2,900-ft.

The hike can be turned into an 11.7-mile loop by taking a right at the Cross Mountain junction and following the Lizard Head trail to the top of Blackface Mountain in 2.4 miles. From here the trail descends to Lizard Head Pass on Highway 145 in 3.8 miles.

Complete the loop by walking west through the parking area to the road leading downhill toward the highway. Follow the road for a short distance. Just before the road reaches the highway you will see an unmarked trail heading right (southwest). Take this unsigned trail, which follows an old railroad grade paralleling the highway for 2.25 miles back to the Cross Mountain trailhead parking area. The total walking distance for the loop is 11.7 miles

Note: the views are better when the loop is done in reverse, starting at the Lizard Head Trail.

For more information see the Lizard Head and Railroad Grade route descriptions.

Driving Directions

From Telluride: Drive south from Telluride on Colorado 145 over Lizard Head Pass (12.5-miles). Continue south for 2.2 miles and turn right onto a dirt road signed for the Cross Mountain trailhead.

25. Old Railroad Grade ★★☆☆☆
Distance: 2.25 miles (one-way)

The 2.25-mile unmarked Railroad Grade route, linking the Cross Mountain trailhead to the Lizard Head trailhead, enables hikers to complete a great 11.7 mile loop over Black Face Mountain to the base of the Lizard Head spire in the Lizard Head Wilderness. The walk may also be of interest to people looking for a nice easy stroll from the Lizard Head Pass parking area or the Cross Mountain trailhead.

Distance: 2.25 miles (one-way)   **Basecamp:** Telluride
Elevation: 10,040-ft. at the trailhead   **Area:** San Juan NF
Maximum Elevation: 10,280-ft.   **Best Season:** July - September
Elevation Gain: 240-ft.   **USGS Map(s):** Mt. Wilson
Difficulty: easy   **See Page 107 for Map**

Trail Description - Old Railroad Grade

One of the great hikes in the Telluride area is the 11.7-mile Lizard Head loop. The trail, which starts just off of Highway 145 at Lizard Head Pass, traverses the panoramic spine of Blackface Mountain on its way to the base of Lizard Head peak (13,113-ft.), an eroded 400-ft tall spire shaped like the gaping maw of a lizard with its face to the sky. At the base of Lizard Head the trail meets the Cross Mountain trail, which drops down to Highway 145 just over 2-miles southwest of the pass.

Hikers complete the loop by walking 2.25 miles back to the Lizard Head trailhead on the unmarked former railroad bed of the Rio Grande Southern Railroad. In its heyday the narrow gauge railroad linked Durango, Colorado to Ridgway, Colorado, crossing 10,222-ft Lizard Head Pass en route to Placerville and ultimately Ridgway over Dallas Divide. The railroad ceased operation in 1951.

Hikers descending the Cross Mountain trail seeking to return to the Lizard Head trailhead should look for a wide, dirt path leading left (northeast) about 0.1 miles before the Cross Mountain trailhead parking area. Follow the unmarked path through meadows as it swings away from the highway to avoid a small drainage. Red metal markers, warning people not to dig in the area due to buried high voltage power lines, appear at intervals along the first half of the route.

The trail ascends gently, essentially paralleling the highway and offering nice views of Black Face Mountain and the peaks around Trout Lake, including Sheep Mountain, Vermilion Peak, Golden Horn and Pilot Knob. As you progress the dirt route turns to grass, but the way is always clear. At 0.9 miles skirt a metal barrier across the trail intended to block further vehicle access.

In slightly over a mile from the start the trail levels out and only experiences minor ups and downs for the remainder of the walk. Shortly after this point the trail swings toward the highway and stays about 75-yards from the artery until you reach the access road to the Lizard Head Pass parking area. Walk up the access road to where you left your vehicle.

For more information on the loop trail see the Lizard Head and Cross Mountain trail descriptions.

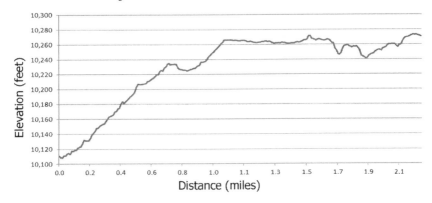

Driving Directions

From Telluride to the Lizard Head Trailhead: Drive south from Telluride on Colorado 145 for 12.3 miles to Lizard Head Pass. On the right (west) side of the highway is a rest area and interpretive site. Turn right into the rest area and park. To find the unmarked trailhead walk to the southwest end of the parking area and proceed down the access road toward the highway. The trail takes off to the right about 100 yards before the road meets Highway 145.

From Telluride to the Cross Mountain Trailhead: Drive south from Telluride on Colorado 145 over Lizard Head Pass (12.5-miles). Continue south for 2.2 miles and turn right onto a dirt road signed for the Cross Mountain trailhead. Walk up the Cross Mountain trail for about 0.1 miles and look for a wide, unmarked dirt track heading left (northeast). This is the railroad grade route.

26. Navajo Lake Trail ★★★★★
Distance: 9.2 miles (RT)

This popular hike climbs through forest and meadows to a stark alpine lake basin surrounded by high peaks in the Lizard Head Wilderness.

Distance: 9.2 miles (RT)
Elevation: 9,320-ft. at Trailhead
11,154-ft. at Navajo Lake
Elevation Gain: 1,834-ft.
Difficulty: moderate-strenuous

Basecamp: Telluride
Area: Lizard Head Wilderness,
San Juan NF
Best Season: July - September
USGS Map(s): Dolores Peak

Why Navajo Lake

The West Dolores River originates at the head of Navajo Basin, a stark elongate glacial bowl lined by steep 13,000-ft. plus ridges. Gladstone Peak (13,913-ft.) dominates the head of the basin while El Diente (14,159-ft.) and Mount Wilson (14,017) rear above the bowl's south ridge. Wilson Peak (14,246-ft.) serves as the terminus for the basin's northern wall.

Nestled deep in the lower end of the basin is scenic Navajo Lake (11,154-ft.). The trail to the lake climbs the broad valley formed by the West Dolores River before steeply ascending to the lake. En route the trail travels through forests, passes waterfalls and traverses beautiful wildflower-filled meadows with good views of Dolores Peak (13,290-ft.) and El Diente.

You'll not be alone on the trail. Navajo Lake is a popular destination for day hikers, backpackers and climbers. Peak baggers use the lake as a base camp to summit the nearby fourteeners. If you do not mind company, a hike to the lake is well worth the effort.

Trailhead to Kilpacker Trail Junction

Distance from Trailhead: 2.2 miles (one-way)
Elevation: 10,190-ft.
Elevation Gain: 870-ft.

There are two access routes to Navajo Lake from the south, the Navajo Lake Trail and the Kilpacker Trail, which meet and share the final 2.4 miles to the lake. The Navajo Lake trail is shorter and the lower portion of the trail is more scenic. The Kilpacker trail starts higher (10,060-ft.) and does not involve as much elevation gain. (See the Kilpacker Trail description in this guide for more information.)

From the Navajo Lake trailhead (see driving directions below) follow the trail up the right (east) side of the West Dolores River past the Groundhog trail, which heads left (west) on a footbridge crossing the River. In less than a mile the trail crosses to the west side of the river on a bridge.

The trail now climbs above the river on moderate grades, traveling through wildflower-filled meadows and intermittent groves of mixed conifers. Views from the meadows include Dolores Peak (13,290-ft.) to the northwest and El Diente (14,159-ft.) to the east. After gaining 870-ft. in a little over 2.2 miles the trail meets the Kilpacker trail (coming in from the east) in a large meadow. The junction is marked with a small sign.

Kilpacker Junction to Navajo Lake

Segment Stat: 2.4 miles (one-way) with a 964-ft. elevation gain
Distance - Trailhead to Navajo Lake: 9.2 miles (RT)
Elevation Navajo Lake: 11,154-ft.
Elevation Gain - Trailhead to Navajo Lake: 1,834-ft.

Beyond the junction the trail ascends, steeply at times, through forest and meadows toward the head of the valley. The meadows offer nice views to the northeast of El Diente's rust-colored western ridge and the ridge defining Navajo Basin's northern wall.

At 3.1 miles the trail starts a steep climb up the valley's north wall. The trail breaks from the trees at 3.4 miles and ascends a series of steep switchbacks through meadows sprinkled with wildflowers and dispersed groups of trees to the junction with the Woods Lake trail at 4.0 miles, gaining 870-ft. over 0.9 miles. Turn right (east) at the signed junction toward Navajo Lake.

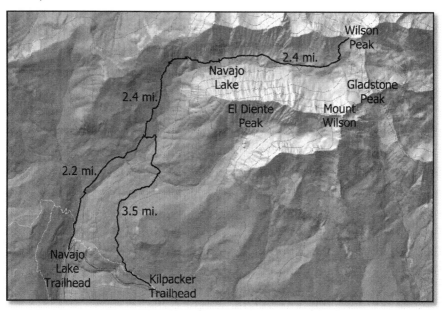

The trail climbs slightly, then drops 160-ft. and then climbs again to reach the western shore of Navajo Lake (11,154-ft) at 4.6 miles. The lake sits in a stark basin ringed by steep, rugged ridges. Gladstone Peak (13,913) rises above the headwall at the eastern end of the basin. El Diente (14,159-ft.) and Mount Wilson loom above the basin's south rim, hidden from view by steep scree slopes. Wilson Peak (14,017) anchors the head of the basin's northern wall but is also concealed from view.

This is the end of the day hike for most people. Backpackers camping at the lake and day hikers with excess energy (and good weather) can continue on the trail along the north side of the lake. Beyond the lake the trail climbs talus slopes to reach the upper end of the basin where it turns left (northwest) and climbs switchbacks up to the Rock of Ages saddle (13,000-ft.) and the junction with the new Rock of Ages trail, gaining 1,846-ft. in 2.4 miles. Total round trip from the Navajo Lake trailhead to the saddle is 14.0 miles.

Driving Directions

From Telluride: Drive south from Telluride on Colorado 145 for 17.9 miles and turn right onto the Dunton Road (#207). The turnoff is located 5.4 miles south of Lizard Head Pass. The narrow gravel and dirt road ascends the hillside on a switchback and then traverses the northeast side of the Coal Creek drainage, crossing the creek in a little under 4 miles.

Continue on the Dunton Road and turn right (north) at the marked entrance for the Navajo Lake trailhead (7 miles from the intersection with Colorado 145). The turn off is located just beyond a sharp left curve in the road. Drive 0.1 miles to the parking area.

27. Kilpacker Trail to Navajo Lake ★★★★★
Distance: 11.5 miles (RT)

This alternative route travels through forest and then joins the Navajo Lake trail, a popular hike to a pretty alpine lake basin surrounded by high peaks. The combined route involves less elevation gain then the Navajo Lake trail but is 2.6 miles (RT) longer.

Distance: 11.8 miles (RT) to Navajo Lake
Elevation: 10,060-ft. at Trailhead 11,154-ft. at Navajo Lake
Elevation Gain: 1,094-ft. to Navajo Lake
Difficulty: moderate-strenuous

Basecamp: Telluride
Area: Lizard Head Wilderness, San Juan NF
Best Season: July - September
USGS Map(s): Dolores Peak
See Page 115 for Map

Why Hike Kilpacker Trail to Navajo Lake

There are two access routes to the Navajo Lake basin from the south, the Navajo Lake trail and the Kilpacker trail. The two trails meet and share the final 2.6 miles of the Navajo Lake trail to the lake.

The Kilpacker trail starts higher (10,060-ft. versus 9,320-ft.) and does not involve as much elevation gain, but is longer adding 1.3 miles to the one way distance. (The Kilpacker Trail replaces the initial 2.2 miles of the Navajo Lake trail with a 3.5 mile segment.) It should be noted that the Kilpacker trail loses elevation to reach the Navajo Lake trail junction, making the net elevation difference about 520-ft.

Views on the Navajo Lake trail are better, steadily improving as you climb. The Kilpacker trailhead, located in a large meadow to the west of Morgan Camp, initially features great views of the surrounding peaks as it heads northwest through the meadows. At 0.6 miles the trail enters a mixed conifer forest with only occasional views until it meets the Navajo Lake trail.

Trailhead to Junction with Navajo Lake

Distance from Trailhead: 3.5 miles (one-way)
Elevation: 10,190-ft.
Elevation Gain/Loss: 404-ft. / -274-ft.

The Kilpacker trail starts at a large sign board in the meadow west of Morgan Camp. Follow the trail as it gently climbs west/northwest through meadows and enters a mixed conifer forest. The easy walk through the forest traverses an undulating landscape in and out of minor drainages. At 2.3 miles reach a trail junction and turn left (west) on the Kilpacker trail. (The trail continuing straight ahead leads to Kilpacker Basin and is used by climbers to reach El Diente and Wilson Peaks.)

The trail now drops through trees and intermittent meadows, losing 274-ft. over the 0.9 miles on its way to the West Dolores River. Cross the river on logs and follow the trail uphill for 0.2 miles to the signed junction with the Navajo Lake trail. Turn right (north) toward the lake basin.

Junction to Navajo Lake

Segment Stat: 2.4 miles (one-way) with a 964-ft. elevation gain
Distance - Trailhead to Navajo Lake: 11.8 miles (RT)
Elevation Navajo Lake: 11,154-ft.
Elevation Gain - Trailhead to Navajo Lake: 1,094-ft.

Beyond the junction the trail ascends, steeply at times, through forest and meadows toward the head of the valley. The meadows offer nice views to the northeast of El Diente's rust-colored western ridge and the ridge defining Navajo Basin's northern wall.

At 4.4 miles the trail starts a steep climb up the valley's north wall. The trail breaks from the trees at 4.7 miles and ascends a series of steep

117

switchbacks through meadows sprinkled with wildflowers and dispersed groups of trees to the junction with the Woods Lake trail at 5.3 miles, gaining 870-ft. over 0.9 miles. Turn right (east) at the signed junction toward Navajo Lake.

The trail climbs slightly, then drops 160-ft. and then climbs again to reach the western shore of Navajo Lake (11,154-ft) at 5.9 miles. The lake sits in a stark basin ringed by steep, rugged ridges. Gladstone Peak (13,913) rises above the headwall at the eastern end of the basin. El Diente (14,159-ft.) and Mount Wilson loom above the basin's south rim, hidden from view by steep scree slopes. Wilson Peak (14,017) anchors the head of the basin's northern wall but is also concealed from view.

This is the end of the day hike for most people. Backpackers camping at the lake and day hikers with excess energy (and good weather) can continue on the trail along the north side of the lake. Beyond the lake the trail climbs talus slopes to reach the upper end of the basin where it turns left (northwest) and climbs switchbacks up to the Rock of Ages saddle (13,000-ft.) and the junction with the new Rock of Ages trail, gaining 1,846-ft. in 2.4 miles. Total round trip from the Navajo Lake trailhead to the saddle is 14.0 miles.

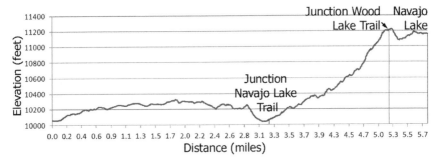

Driving Directions

From Telluride: Drive south from Telluride on Colorado 145 for 17.9 miles and turn right onto the Dunton Road (#207). The turnoff is located 5.4 miles south of Lizard Head Pass. The gravel and dirt road ascends the hillside on a switchback and then traverses the northeast side of the Coal Creek drainage, crossing the creek in a little under 4 miles.

To reach the Kilpacker Trailhead follow the Dunton Road from the intersection with Colorado 145 for a 5.1 miles. Just past Morgan Camp watch for a dirt road on your right (north side of the road). Turn right and follow the road a short distance past a group of trees to an obvious parking area. The trailhead, designated with a large information board, is located to the west of the parking area.

28. Liberty Bell/Marshall Basin ★★★★★
Distance: 6.2 - 10.6 miles (loop)

This lightly traveled trail climbs steeply to Liberty Bell basin and a scenic ridge. Extend the hike by descending through Marshall Basin, scattered with mining ruins, on an off trail route to the Tomboy Mine and ghost town. Complete the loop by walking the Tomboy Road back to town.

Distance: 7.2 miles (RT) to Liberty Basin and Divide
6.0 miles (one way) to Marshall Basin/Tomboy Mine
10.6 miles (loop) to Telluride
Elevation: 8,880-ft. at Trailhead
12,575-ft. at Liberty Basin Divide
11,400-ft. at Marshall Basin/Tomboy Mine
8,800-ft. at Telluride
Elevation Gain: 3,695-ft. to Liberty Basin Divide
-1,175-ft. to Marshall Basin/Tomboy Mine
-2,520-ft. to Telluride

Difficulty: strenuous
Basecamp: Telluride
Area: Uncompahgre NF
Best Season: July - September
USGS Map(s): Telluride
See Page 80 for Map

Why Hike Liberty Bell / Marshall Basins

This varied hike, off the beaten track, offers walkers a good workout, great views and an opportunity to see ruins of the two top producing mining operations in the Upper San Miguel Mining District – the Smuggler-Union and Tomboy mines.

From downtown Telluride a good trail with limited views climbs steeply to Liberty Bell basin. For the first mile the trail travels along the Tomboy Road and the Jud Wiebe Trail. Beyond this point you will see few people until you reach the Tomboy Mine.

At the foot of the basin a steep trail ascends to the ridge separating the Liberty Bell and Marshall basins. As you climb to the ridge enjoy great views of Greenback Mountain (12,997-ft.), Mount Emma (13,581-ft.), the Saint Sophia ridge and, in the distance, the high peaks of the Lizard Head Wilderness. Atop the ridge views extend down the length of the Marshall Basin. Savage Basin and the road snaking to Imogene are visible to the southeast.

Hikers comfortable with off-trail route finding can extend the hike by heading down the east side of the ridge into the Marshall Basin where the discovery of the Smuggler Vein in 1875 led to the formation of the Smuggler-Union mine in 1887-1889. Today remnants of the large mining operation are scatter about the valley.

119

The off-trail route soon connects with old mining roads that descend the basin and intersect the Tomboy Road just below the Tomboy Mine. A short walk up the Tomboy Road leads to the substantial ruins of the Tomboy Mine at the foot of Savage Basin. About 900 people lived and worked at the mine during the late 1800's to early 1900's. Wander a further half mile up the road to see a ghost town and more mining structures.

The loop trail returns to Telluride along the Tomboy Road. The ruins of interesting mining structures along with great views of the Savage Basin, Bridal Veil Basin and Falls, the Bear Creek Valley and the town of Telluride will help you to forget you are walking along a road back to town.

Be advised that the off-trail section of the loop descends very steep grass and talus slopes. When passing through the basin please view the mine ruins from a distance. Exploring tailings, mine shafts and unstable building is extremely dangerous. The ruins of the Tomboy Townsite are on private property, please do not trespass.

Trailhead to Liberty Basin and Divide

Distance from Trailhead: 3.6 miles (one-way) / 7.2 miles (RT)
Ending/Highest Elevation: 12,575-ft.
Elevation Gain: 3,695-ft.

From the north end of Oak Street (see directions to the trailhead below), turn right (east) on the Tomboy Road and walk up the jeep road for 0.4 miles to the Jud Wiebe trail (eastern trailhead) on the left (north) side of the road. There is a metal gate and a sign board marking the trail.

Turn left (northwest) on the Jud Wiebe trail (#432) and follow the broad dirt track as it climbs steep switchbacks up the north side of the Telluride valley, passing the town's water storage tanks. The trail initial ascends through meadows with nice views of Telluride and the ski area across the valley before entering the forest.

After walking about a mile the grade abates as the trail enters the Cornet Creek Valley and soon reaches a signed junction at Liberty Bell Flats. Here the Jud Wiebe Trail branches left (west). We bear right (northeast) on the Liberty Bell trail (#870). After a short stint through a pretty glade of aspens the steep climb resumes up the east side of the Cornet Valley.

The trail, actually an old road, travels through trees, crosses a creek and arrives at an unsigned junction at 1.8 miles. Keep right at the intersection to stay on the Liberty Bell trail. The track to the left provides access to the Stillwell Tunnel which channels water to the storage tanks passed earlier.

At 2.0 miles pass the remains of an old cabin and other structures on the left. Beyond the ruins the trail climbs a switchback and then crosses a meadow with views of the peaks towering above the head the Telluride valley. Wilson Peak (14,017-ft.), Mount Wilson (14,246-ft.), El Diente (14,159-ft.), Sunshine Mountain (12,930-ft.) and Lizard Head (13,113-ft.) in the Lizard Head Wilderness fill the skyline to the southwest.

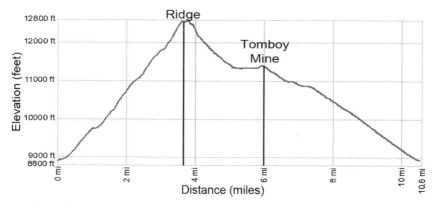

The views are short lived. Soon the trail plunges back into the trees and continues its relentless climb, crossing a minor ridge along the way. Occasional openings in the trees offer glimpses of the peaks rimming the Cornet Valley.

At 2.7 miles the trail turns right (east/southeast) and climbs steeply up a series switchbacks, reaching Liberty Bell basin at 3.1 miles. Here the trees give way to meadows with great views of Greenback Mountain (12,997-ft.) and Mount Emma (13,581-ft.) rising above the head of the Cornet valley. The jagged profile of the St. Sophia Ridge, extending southeast from Mt. Emma, dominates the view to the north.

As you enter the basin the road curves to the right (south). Here you will see a trail heading east (essentially straight ahead) and climbing the basin to the ridge separating Liberty Bell Basin and Marshall Basin. A large rock cairn marks the intersection.

If time and energy allow, I recommend hiking to the ridge. The trail initially ascends along the north side of a line of trees and then curve to the left as it climbs through pretty alpine meadows dotted with wildflowers in season. At 3.5 miles the trail hits the scree slopes beneath the ridge and arcs to the right. Exercise care where the narrow trail crosses a few small slides.

Reach the top of the ridge 3.6 miles. Terrific views extend northwest toward Mt. Emma. Dallas Peak (13,741-ft.) rises to the west. The peaks of the Lizard Head Wilderness dominate the view to the southwest. On the east side of the pass views extend down the length of the Marshall Basin. Savage Basin and the road snaking to Imogene are visible to the southeast.

At this point parties can turn around and retrace their steps back to Telluride for a 7.2 mile round-trip hike or descend the Marshall Basin to the Tomboy Mine and then walk back to Telluride along the Tomboy Road. If you like old mine sites and mining ruins your will love the Marshall Basin and the Tomboy mine. The walk, which includes an off trail segment with very steep grades, also includes great views of the Marshall and Savage basins and the Telluride box canyon. The final segment travels along the Tomboy Road, which is not heavily traveled, especially if you avoid the weekends.

To Marshall Basin and the Tomboy Mine

Distance from Trailhead: 6.0 miles (one way)
Ending/Highest Elevation: 11,400-ft.
Elevation Gain: -1,175-ft.

In 1875 John Fallon discovered what is now known as the Smuggler Vein in the upper Marshall Basin. The next year J.B. Ingram and two others staked a claimed called the Smuggler in the lower section of the basin. The mines along the Smuggler Vein consolidated to form the Smuggler-Union Mining Co. twelve years later. These mines, along with the Tomboy Gold Mine in neighboring Savage Basin, were the top producing companies in the San Miguel Mining district until the claims played out in the 1920's.

The second half of this loop hike descends through the Marshall Basin, passing the ruins of these mining operations. From the ridge follow the boot beaten path heading northeast along scree clad slopes into Marshall Basin. Use care on the short sections of the trail that cross minor slide areas.

Soon the rocky slopes give way to meadows and the walking is easier. As you look ahead you will see the trail climbing the scree slopes to the north as the trail heads for Virginus Pass, a small notch on the ridge. This pass leads to Governor's Basin, accessed from Ouray along the Yankee Boy basin road.

After 0.25 miles the trail crosses two small drainages. Ahead you will see the trail start to climb toward the head of the basin. I typically leave the trail here and descend about 100-ft before crossing the drainage to the east side of the basin.

(Note: There are vestiges of a trail dropping down the west side of the Marshall Basin. In the past I have found parts of this route obliterated by slides/avalanches. I now prefer the route described below.)

Once on the east side of the drainage descend the basin on very steep grassy slopes, skirting the mine tailings and talus fields in the middle of the basin. The goal is to drop down to the next level of the basin and then cross back to the west side of the valley between the two huge tailings piles scattered with mine debris.

As you descend you will see a white cement drainage ditch built to control runoff from the defunct mine. Cross to the west side of the basin above this ditch, selecting a route that avoids crossing tailings piles and other debris. Descend the west side of the basin, staying to the right (west) of the cement drainage ditch until you hit an old road.

Follow the road down the basin, past more tailing piles and mine ruins. At 4.6 miles the road crosses the cement ditch. On the other side of the ditch follow a gravel road that curves to the left (east) and soon crosses a stream. Across the stream turn right (southeast) on a gravel road and follow the road as it descending along the east side of the basin to meet the Tomboy Road at 5.8 miles, just below the Tomboy Mine. This section of the hike will pass the remains of interesting mining structures including the remains of the tramway.

Turn left (east) at the Tomboy road and walk a short distance up the road to the substantial ruins of the Tomboy mine at 6.0 miles, located at the foot of Savage Basin. In its heyday, during the late 1800's and early 1900's, about 900 people lived and worked at the mine. When the ore ran out in 1927 the town went bust and was soon abandoned.

Ghost town enthusiasts will want to wander a half mile up the road to see the remains of the ghost town and more mining structures. Beyond the last structures the road climbs to Imogene Pass (13,114-ft.), a total distance of 2.2 miles from the main ruins at the foot of the basin.

From Tomboy Mine to Telluride

Distance from Trailhead: 10.6 miles (loop)
Ending/Highest Elevation: 8,800-ft.
Elevation Gain: -2,520-ft.

When you are done exploring the mine follow the Tomboy Road back to Telluride. There is some traffic on the road. A few Telluride tour operators run half day tours to the Tomboy Mine and Imogene Pass. Skilled 4WD enthusiasts like to drive the rough road over Imogene Pass, typically starting in Telluride and ending in Ouray. Most like to get over Imogene Pass early in the day to beat any afternoon thunderstorms, which can make the road impassable. As such, traffic tends to be lighter in the afternoon when most hikers will be completing this portion of the loop.

From the mine the road descends to Telluride on moderate to easy grades, traveling above the north side of Savage Creek. At 6.7 miles you will see an old cabin perched above the north side of the road. Beyond the cabin the road crosses a bridge over Marshall Creek and then head southwest high above the north side of Marshall Creek. Ruins and debris of an old tramway are visible below the road. Behind you are nice views up Savage Basin.

At 6.9 miles pass the Bullion Tunnel and the remnants of the Smuggler-Union mine, which includes the ruins of a crusher house and a multistory boarding house, which has now slid down the hill. Nearby are two large boilers, pipes and cables from the tramway that once carried ore to the Pandora Mill, located in the Telluride Valley.

As you continue down the road nice views open to Bridal Veil Falls and the Bridal Veil Basin at the head of Telluride's box canyon.

At 7.6 miles the trail curves to the right (west), leaving the Marshall Creek Valley and now travels high above the north side of the Telluride valley.

Pass through a tunnel on the road at 7.9 miles. This is a popular spot for photographers.

Beyond the tunnel the road curves into and out of Rover Gulch. Near the head of the gulch are some nice waterfalls cascading down the cliffs above the road. As the road exits the gulch it heads down two long switchbacks. Across the valley to the south nice views of Bear Creek Valley. Behind you views stretch southeast to Bridal Veil Falls and the peaks rising above the head of the Telluride Valley.

The final section of the trail follows a long descending traverse above the town, passing the Jud Wiebe trail junction at 10.2 miles and reaching the top of Oak Street at 10.6 miles.

Driving Directions

Driving Directions from Telluride: Note: Free day-use parking in Telluride is available in the Carhenge Lot just off West Pacific Avenue at the west end of town near the base of Lift 7. Day use parking for larger vehicles is available in the parking lot at the south end of Mahoney Drive, near the west entrance to town. A free shuttle bus, called the Galloping Goose, runs between the parking lots and various stops in downtown Telluride.

There is also free parking in the mountain village lot. From there you can take the free gondola into town and easily walk to the trailhead.

Walking directions: From Telluride's main street (Colorado Avenue), turn north onto Aspen Street and proceed one block. Turn right (east) onto Columbia Avenue and proceed one block. Turn left (north) onto Oak Street and walk to the end of the street. Turn right (east) on the Tomboy Road, a good dirt road.

29. Handies Peak ★★★★★

Distance:2.3 - 5.4 miles (RT)

This terrific hike wanders through beautiful American Basin, visits scenic Sloan Lake and then ascends to the summit of Handies Peak (14,048-ft.) with spectacular panoramic views of the San Juan Mountains.

Distance: 2.3 miles (RT) to Sloan Lake
5.4 miles (RT) to Handies Peak
Elevation: 11,600-ft. at Trailhead
12,920-ft. at Sloan Lake
14,048-ft. at Handies Peak
Elevation Gain: 1,320-ft. to Sloan Lake
2,448-ft. to Handies Peak

Difficulty: strenuous
Basecamp: Lake City
Area: Gunnison BLM
Best Season: July - September
USGS Map(s): Handies Peak

Why Hike Handies Peak

The stunning panoramic views from the top of Handies Peak (14,048-ft.) are among the best in the Lake City area. From the summit a large expanse of a the San Juan Mountains are visible including the Needle Mountains, the Grenadier Range, the La Garita Mountains and the peaks of the Uncompahgre and Mt. Sneffel Wilderness Areas.

The hike to the summit is filled with visual delights. The trail wanders through beautiful American Basin, one of the most scenic valleys in the San Juan Mountains. The entire basin, located above timberline, is covered in pretty meadows that are awash in a spectacular display of wildflowers during late July and early August. An impressive chain of craggy peaks towers above the head of the basin while the valley's eastern wall is dominated by the massive bulk of Handies Peak (14,048-ft.). Rising to the west are the steep flanks of 13,000-ft. peaks clad in tundra and scree.

At the head of the valley the route climbs to picturesque Sloan Lake (12,920-ft.), an alpine gem tucked in a rocky bowl beneath the valley's rugged headwall.

While the hike to Handies is steep, gaining almost 2,500-ft. in 2.7 miles, it follows a good trail the entire way and is not difficult. Indeed the peak is considered one of the easiest of the fourteeners to climb in the Lake City Area. Well acclimated and reasonably fit hiker should have no problems reaching to top.

Be sure to select a day full of promise and get an early start so you can take your time enjoying the incredible views from the top and descend before the onset of afternoon thunder storms, a frequent occurrence in the Rockies.

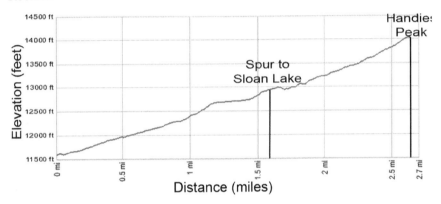

Trailhead to Sloan Lake

Distance from Trailhead: 2.3 miles (RT)
Ending/Highest Elevation: 12,920-ft.
Elevation Gain: 1,320-ft.

Few trailheads boast the impressive scenery at the start of the hike to Handies Peak. From the parking area views extend south across the basin's emerald green meadows to the rugged 13,000-ft. ridge towering above the head of the valley. The scenery is especially impressive during late July and early August when a showy display of wildflowers carpets the valley floor.

The Handies Peak trail leaves the southeast end of the trailhead parking area and ascends the hillside on the left (east) side of the valley, heading south into the basin through pretty meadows. At 0.7 miles the path crosses a stream and then continues the moderate ascent toward the head of the basin.

At 1.0 mile the trail splits. The path to Handies Peak turns left (southeast), leaving the valley floor and climbs 325-ft up a moderately steep hillside. At the top of hill the path descends into a shallow basin, crosses the outlet stream for Sloan Lake and then follows a gently ascending grade across rocky meadows. Soon the path turns south, climbing steep switchbacks 200-ft up to a junction with the trail to Sloan Lake at 1.6 miles. At the junction a short spur trail drops south to the shores of Sloan Lake (12,930-ft.) while the trail to Handies Peak veers left.

The short side trip to Sloan Lake is well worth your time. The aquamarine lake lies cradled in a rugged cirque, anchored to the southeast by American Peak (13,806-ft.). An imposing jagged ridge rises above the lake's south shoreline.

Sloan Lake to Handies Peak

Distance from Trailhead: 5.4 miles (RT)
Ending/Highest Elevation: 14,048-ft.
Elevation Gain: 2,448-ft.

To continue hiking to the summit return to the junction and follow the trail as it curves to the northeast, traversing the talus slopes beneath an unnamed peak on the ridge extending south from Handies Peak. The traverse leads to the southwest facing flank of Handies Peak where a series of steep switchbacks ascend grassy meadows to the 13,490-ft. saddle on the peak's south ridge, gaining 460-ft. in 0.5 miles.

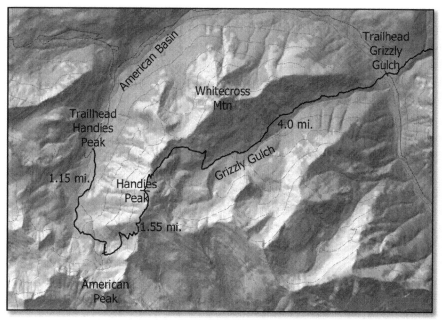

The way to the summit is now evident. Follow the trail is it steeply ascends the south ridge on scree covered slopes, gaining 560-ft in 0.4 miles.

The panoramic views from the top are some of the best in the area. To the southwest the jagged peaks of the Grenadier Range and Needles Mountains extend to the horizon. To the north are the distinctive summits of the Uncompahgre Wilderness, including Wetterhorn, Matterhorn and Uncompahgre Peaks. To the northeast is the La Garita Range while to the west/northwest the peaks of the San Juan Mountains near Silverton and Ouray, including the Mt. Sneffels Range, fill the skyline.

After taking in the views retrace your steps back to your car. Alternatively, combine the Handies Peak trail with the Grizzly Gulch trail to form a long, strenuous loop. The loop can be hiked in either direction. Many people start at the Grizzly Gulch trailhead and hike up to Handies Peak. From the top follow the Handies Peak trail down through American Basin to the main road and back to the Grizzly Gulch Trailhead. This 10 mile loop gains 3,592-ft.

Driving Directions

Driving Directions from Lake City: Take Highway 149 south for 2.5 miles and turn right (south) on County Road 30 toward the Lake San Cristobal. Follow the paved road approximately 4 miles and then continue on the dirt road for about 16.3 miles. The American Basin road begins at a fork where a sign reads "Cinnamon Pass/American Basin". American Basin is to the left and Cinnamon Pass is to the right. Turn left and follow the rough 4WD road, with one stream crossing, for 0.9 miles to the trailhead.

High clearance passenger cars should be able to make it to the American Basin turnoff. Check with the tourism office in Lake City on current road conditions before starting your journey.

30. Uncompahgre Peak ★★★★★
Distance: 7.8 miles (RT)

Stunning panoramic views are the rewards for hiking to the top Uncompahgre Peak (14,309-ft.), the sixth highest fourteener in Colorado and the highest point in the San Juan Mountains.

Distance: 7.8 miles (RT)
Elevation: 11,430-ft. at Trailhead
Maximum elevation: 14,309-ft.
Elevation Gain: 2,879-ft.
Difficulty: strenuous-difficult

Basecamp: Lake City
Area: Uncompahgre Wilderness, Uncompahgre NF
Best Season: July - September
USGS Map(s): Uncompahgre Peak

Why Hike Uncompahgre Peak

The uniquely shaped summit block of Uncompahgre Peak (14,309-ft.) is a well know landmark in the San Juan Mountains. From a distance the peak looks like a formidable climb but the ascent up the mountain's south ridge is quite doable for hikers that are well acclimated and reasonably fit.

Hiking to the summit is well worth the effort. For most of the way the trail climbs through beautiful meadows with unobstructed views of the peak's south and east faces. Beyond the meadows the trail ascends Uncompahgre's south ridge. As you approach the summit there is one short, steep scramble before you get back on a good trail for the final stiff climb to the top. The broad summit, which stands apart from the surrounding peaks, offers stunning panoramic views in all directions.

Pick a nice day and get an early start so that you are down from the summit before the onset of afternoon thunder storms, a frequent occurrence in the Rockies. Also, be forewarned that the final 4.0 miles drive to the trailhead is up the rough and narrow Nellie Creek 4WD road. Do not even think about taking a passenger car up this road.

Walking up the Nellie Creek road will add 8 miles (RT) and 2,115-ft. to the climb making this a 15.8 mile (RT) hike with an elevation gain just under 5,000-ft.

Trailhead to Uncompahgre Peak

The trail starts at the northeast end of the trailhead parking area (see driving directions below) and ascends northwest on moderate grades through meadows and spruce-fir forest, staying to the right (northeast) of Nellie Creek. At 0.6 miles the trail leaves the last of the trees behind and enters a rocky gully where it climbs switchbacks up the gully's north wall to a trail junction with the Big Blue trail ay 0.9 miles.

At the junction the Big Blue trail heads right (north). We turn left (west) on the trail to Uncompahgre Peak. Ahead are stunning, unobstructed views of Uncompahgre's east face and distinctive summit block, which from this angle looks somewhat like a huge lopsided wedding cake.

Follow the trail as it traverses along the top of the gully's north wall. In a short distance you will see Nellie Creek tumbling down a rocky cleft in the wall. At this point the trail starts curving northwest, climbing through the pretty meadows with ever improving views of Uncompahgre Peak. Vistas to the south extend to the peaks rising above the Henson Creek valley.

At 2.0 miles the trail swings south, heading toward the southern end of the basin. Reach a junction (12,940-ft.) at 2.4 miles. Here the the El Paso Trail branches left (southeast) toward Matterhorn Creek. Bear right at the junction to stay on the Uncompahgre trail. From this point you still have 1.5 miles and a 1,370-ft. climb to the summit.

Beyond the junction the trail makes a wide arc to the northwest, heading toward the Uncompahgre's south ridge and then ascends steeply along the east side of the south ridge.

At 3.1 miles a low point in the ridge provides interesting, albeit restricted views of Matterhorn Peak to the west. Past the viewpoint the trail climbs steep switchbacks up a rocky east facing hillside to the crest of the south ridge (13,860-ft.) at 3.4 miles. At the crest take a breather and enjoy the wonderful views of Matterhorn and Wetterhorn Peaks, Courthouse Mountain and the other summits rising to the west.

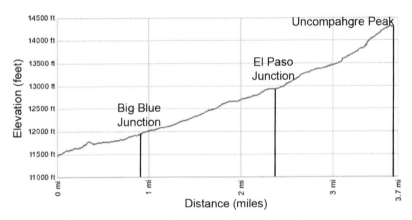

The trail now crosses to the west side of the ridge for a short traverse along a narrow, rocky trail with enough exposure to make some people uncomfortable. Next comes to the most difficult part of the hike, a 125-ft. scramble up a steep eroded slope of loose rock. There are several routes climbing the slope. Pick the way that looks best to you and scramble to the top of the ridge.

At the top of the ridge be sure to turn around and note where you ascended the ridge so you can find your way back down on the return. There should be rock cairns marking the best place to descend.

Once atop the ridge the going is much easier. Follow the trail as heads north/northeast, climbing 340-ft. up a steep scree covered slope to the large plateau at the top of the peak.

Uncompahgre Peak stands apart from its surrounding summits, providing breathtaking vistas in all directions. Expansive views to the west encompass Matterhorn and Wetterhorn Peaks and, in the distance, the summits of the Mt. Sneffels Wilderness. To the north/northwest are the peaks and valleys of the Uncompahgre Wilderness. To the south/southwest the peaks and ridges of the San Juan Mountains fill the skyline.

When you are done soaking in the views, reverse course and enjoy the scenic hike back to the trailhead.

At the top remember to keep an eye on the weather. If thunderstorms are building it is best to descend and head back to the trailhead.

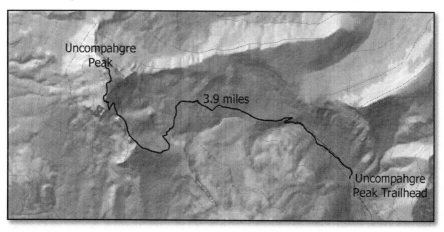

Driving Directions

Driving Directions from Lake City: Head west on Second Street and then turn left onto the Henson Creek Road, part of the Alpine Loop Scenic Byway. Follow Henson Creek Road for 4.0 miles to the Nellie Creek jeep road. Turn right (north) on the Nellie Creek Road and drive for 4 miles to the trailhead up the rough, narrow 4WD road. The road crosses Nellie Creek twice on its way to the trailhead. Do not even think about taking a passenger car on this road.

Walking up the Nellie Creek road will add 8 miles (RT) and 2,115-ft. to the climb, making this a 15.8 mile (RT) hike with an elevation gain just under 5,000-ft.

31. Cataract Lake (aka Cataract Gulch) ★★★★★
Distance: 7.6 - 8.2 miles (RT)

Beginning in dense woods the trail passes cascades and waterfalls along Cataract Creek, travels through beautiful alpine meadows and visits a scenic alpine lake on its way to the Continental Divide.

Distance: 7.6 - 8.2 miles (RT)
Elevation: 9,630-ft. at Trailhead
Maximum elevation: - 12,200-ft.
Elevation Gain: 2,570-ft.
Difficulty: moderate-strenuous

Basecamp: Lake City
Area: Gunnison BLM
Best Season: July - September
USGS Map(s): Red Cloud Peak, Pole Creek Mountain

Why Hike Cataract Lake

This scenic hike climbs steeply up Cataract Gulch to a pretty lake basin just below the Continental Divide. Along the way the trail ascends through dense woods, passes numerous cascades and waterfalls along Cataract Creek and traverses lovely alpine meadows. A potential off-trail connection to Cuba Gulch extends the trip into an overnight backpack.

Trailhead to Cataract Lake and the Continental Divide

Just beyond the trailhead parking area the trail up Cataract Gulch crosses Cottonwood Creek on a bridge and then begins a steep ascent on switchbacks through dense stands of spruce-fir forest. As you climb the trail crosses Cataract Creek five times without the aid of bridges. Generally these crossing are not a problem although you should be prepared to get your feet wet.

During the first 2.0-miles of the hike the trail gains over 2,000-ft. Waterfalls and cascades along Cataract Creek, spectacular displays of wildflowers and an old miner's cabin will help divert your attention from the steep climb. Be sure to turn around when you get to openings in the trees for nice views of Sunshine Peak (14,001-ft.), located to the north (down canyon) across the Lake Fork Valley.

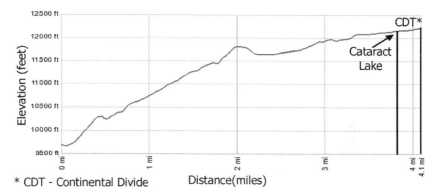

* CDT - Continental Divide

At 2.0 miles the grade eases a bit as the trail climbs through meadows with patches of low lying shrubs. Along this section of the trail views open to Half Peak (13,841-ft.) rising to the west of the trail.

After 3.0 miles the trail becomes easier, ascending on gentle grades through alpine meadows past a few small tarns to Cataract Lake (12,100-ft.) at 3.8 miles. The lake lies in a pretty meadow decorated with small patch of scrub willows just below the Continental Divide.

To reach the Continental Divide, follow the trail along the east side of the lake. At the head of the lake the trail curves to the right (southwest), reaching the Divide (12,200-ft.) at 4.1 miles. From the divide views stretch southeast down the West Lost Creek Valley and beyond.

The divide is the turnaround point for day hikers. It is possible to connect with the Cuba Gulch Trail by going west cross country. A map is essential for finding the right route across the 2.0 miles of open tundra to the head of Cuba Gulch. This loop, totaling about 14 miles, is best done as an overnight backpacking trip.

Driving Directions

Driving Directions from Lake City: From Lake City take Highway 149 south for 2.5 miles. Turn right onto the road to Lake San Cristobal. Follow the paved road approximately 4 miles then continue on the dirt road for about 8.3 miles. At the fork in the road turn left toward Sherman and drive 1.4 miles. A sign marks the trailhead on the left (south) side of the road.

32. Grizzly Gulch ★★★★★
Distance: 8.0 miles (RT)

The top of Handies Peak offers breathtaking views of the San Juan Mountains. This alternative route to the summit is longer and more strenuous but less traveled than the more popular trail to Handies Peak via American Basin.

Distance: 8.0 miles (RT)
Elevation: 10,425-ft. at Trailhead
Maximum elevation: 14,048-ft.
Elevation Gain: 3,623-ft.
Difficulty: extremely difficult

Basecamp: Lake City
Area: Gunnison BLM
Best Season: July - September
USGS Map(s): Handies Peak
See Page 127 for Map

Why Hike Grizzly Gulch to Handies Peak

Grizzly Gulch offers an alternative approach to the summit of Handies Peak (14,048-ft.) that is longer and gains more elevation than the more popular hike to the summit via American Basin. The trail ascends the scenic Grizzly Gulch valley and then climbs the north ridge of Handies Peak to the summit. The pristine valley provides a degree of solitude not

usually found on the route up American Basin and the trail is a good alternative for hikers who do not have a 4WD for negotiating the road up American Basin.

The best time to visit the area is late July and early August when the tundra basin below the peak is carpeted with wildflowers. A small alpine lake in the eastern spur of the basin can be reached as an interesting 1/2-mile side trip.

Trailhead to Handies Peak via Grizzly Gulch

From the trailhead (see driving directions below), follow the trail that starts behind the restroom and leads to a bridge crossing the Lake Fork of the Gunnison River. Beyond the bridge the trail heads straight up the valley through spruce, fir and aspen for about 0.75 mile along the north side of the drainage.

The trail now climbs through a series of avalanche shoots interspersed with small groups of trees. At 1.7 miles leave the last of the trees behind and continue the ascent through beautiful meadows with wonderful views of Handies Peak. Soon the trail enters a gorgeous alpine basin and for a brief period follows alongside the creek, crossing it twice. Be sure to look over your shoulder on the way up the basin for beautiful views of the Silver Creek Valley to the northeast.

Just beyond the second creek crossing a sign points right (north) to a long switchback that helps ease the climb up the west side of Handies' north ridge. The ascent to the ridge gains over 1,225-ft in just under 1.1 miles. Along the way the trail curves to the southwest as it climbs through rocky meadows and crosses a large talus fields. A few switchbacks aid the final stiff climb to the ridge crest.

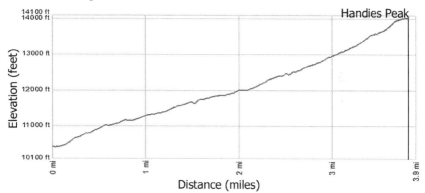

On the ridge the trail heads south, climbing rocky slopes on a series of very steep switchback for 0.2 miles. At the top of the switchbacks the grade abates. The path to the summit is now visible, ascending the ridge crest on moderate grades for 0.2 mile. Reach the top of Handies Peak at 4.0 miles after gaining 3,592-ft.

The panoramic views from the top are some of the best in the area. To the southwest the jagged peaks of the Grenadier Range and Needles Mountains extend to the horizon. To the north are the distinctive summits of the Uncompahgre Wilderness, including Wetterhorn, Matterhorn and Uncompahgre Peaks. To the northeast is the La Garita Range while to the west/northwest the peaks of the San Juan Mountains near Silverton and Ouray, including the Mt. Sneffels Range, fill the skyline.

After taking in the views retrace your steps back to your car. Alternatively combine the Grizzly Gulch trail with the Handies Peak/American Basin trail to create a very scenic 10 mile loop. From the top of Handies Peak take the Handies Peak trail down through American Basin to the main road and back to your car. This 10 mile loop can be done in either direction.

Driving Directions

Driving Directions from Lake City: Take Highway 149 south for 2.5 miles and turn right on County Road 30 toward Lake San Cristobal. Follow the paved road about 4.0 miles then continue on dirt road for 12.6 miles.

Look for a sign on the left (south) side of the road for Handies Peak. Parking is available in defined areas on both sides of the main road.

33. Redcloud and Sunshine Peaks ★★★★★
Distance: 9.0 - 11.8 miles (RT)

This great hike leads to the top of two of the easiest fourteeners to climb in Colorado, Redcloud (14,034 ft.) and Sunshine (14,001 ft.) peaks. From the summits a sea of summits and ridges extend in all directions, encompassing large swaths of the San Juan Mountains.

Distance: 9.0 - 11.8 miles (RT)   **Basecamp:** Lake City
Elevation: 10,425-ft. at Trailhead   **Area:** Gunnison BLM
Maximum elevation: 14,034-ft.   **Best Season:** July - September
Elevation Gain: 3,609-ft.   **USGS Map(s):** Redcloud Peak
Difficulty: extremely difficult

Trailhead to Redcloud and Sunshine Peaks

The trail to Redcloud and Sunshine peaks begins at the Silver Creek trailhead parking area (see driving directions below) and heads northeast, ascending through trees along the west side of the Silver Creek drainage. A little over a mile from the start the trail emerges from the trees and continues up the basin, paralleling the creek. Be sure to turn around during this part of the ascent for ever-improving views of Handies Peak (14,048-ft.) to the southwest.

At 2.7 miles the trail curves to the southeast and climbs to a large basin beneath the north face of Redcloud Peak, reached after hiking 3.1 miles and gaining 1,940-ft. From the basin the path ascends steeply to a saddle on the ridge between Redcloud Peak and Peak 13561, gaining 650-ft. in just over 0.6 miles. Turn right and follow a very steep trail that climbs up the ridge to Redcloud Peak (14,034-ft.). On the way to the peak you will climb over a false summit. This section of the trail gains over 1,000-ft. in just 0.8 miles.

From Redcloud the path to Sunshine Peak descends from the summit along Redcloud's south ridge on an undulating trail, losing about 515-ft. to a saddle between Redcloud and Sunshine. From the saddle the rugged trail climbs 484-ft. up Sunshine's north ridge to Sunshine Peak (14,001-ft.), reaching the peak in a little over 1.4 miles.

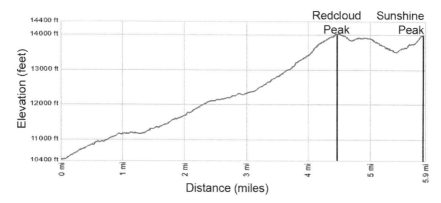

From both summits enjoy panoramic views of a sea of peaks and ridges encompassing large swaths of the San Juan Mountains. To the north Uncompahgre Peak towers above the other summits of the Uncompahgre Wilderness. To the west is a wall of mountains extending from Ouray to Silverton. On a clear day views extend northwest to the Sneffels Range. The Needles and peaks in the Weminuche Wilderness fill the skyline to the south while to the northeast are the 12,000-ft. tundra-clad plateaus of the Powderhorn Wilderness.

Be sure to select a day full of promise and get an early start so you can take your time enjoying the wonderful views from the top and descend before the onset of afternoon thunder storms, a frequent occurrence in the Rockies.

Driving Directions

Driving Directions from Lake City: From Lake City, take Highway 149 south for 2.5 miles and turn right on County Road 30 toward Lake San Cristobal. Follow the paved road approximately 4 miles, then continue on dirt road for 8.3 miles to the fork in the road. Take the right fork (the Alpine Loop Scenic Byway) and drive another 4.2 miles to the trailhead. The trail sign, located on the left, reads

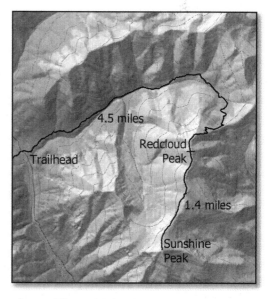

"Redcloud Peak." Under good conditions high clearance 2WD vehicles should be able to reach the trailhead.

34. Devil's Lake (aka Devil's Creek) ★★★★★

Distance: 14.0 miles (RT)

Picturesque groves of mature aspen and beautiful views of the Lake Fork Valley and Uncompahgre Peak are a few of the visual delights on this scenic trail following the Devil's Creek drainage to Devil's Lake, lying beneath the western flanks of the Calf Creek Plateau.

Distance: 14.0 miles (RT) to Devil's Lake
Elevation: 8,480-ft. at Trailhead 12,000-ft. at Devil's Lake
Elevation Gain: 3,520-ft. to Devil's Lake
Difficulty: strenuous

Basecamp: Lake City
Area: Powderhorn Wilderness, Gunnison BLM, Gunnison NF
Best Season: July - September
USGS Map(s): Alpine Plateau, Cannibal Plateau, Powderhorn Lakes, Lake City

Why Hike to Devil's Lake

In the northern reaches of the San Juan Mountains lies the Powderhorn Wilderness, a rugged, glacier carved landscape encompassing large expanses of alpine tundra, spruce forests, and several alpine lakes at nearly 12,000-ft. The wilderness harbors two huge plateaus over 12,000-ft., the Cannibal Plateau and the Calf Creek Plateau, that make up the largest relatively flat expanse of alpine tundra in the lower 48 states. The plateaus were created by Tertiary volcanic deposits that are believed to be 5,000-ft. thick in some place.

This trail climbs the Devil's Creek drainage to Devil's Lake, which lies nestled in a tundra-clad saddle between the Cannibal and Calf Creek

138

Plateaus. Beautiful views of the Lake Fork Valley and Uncompahgre Peak are visible from many points along the trail.

Trailhead to Devil's Lake

From the trailhead parking area (see driving directions below) the trail heads east, climbing an old road to the north of Devil's Creek drainage. Soon the trail leaves the road, climbing switchbacks up the west side of the Lake Fork Gunnison Valley. Along the way the the path will cross and/or use sections of the road. In a little over a mile the trail tops a mesa and then gently ascends across the sage brush clad mesa top before turning northeast through a fence line and into the Powderhorn Wilderness at 1.5 miles. From the mesa nice views extend west to the peaks and ridges of the Uncompahgre Wilderness.

Over the next mile the trail again departs from and returns to the old road several times, traversing through pretty stands of aspen and spruce-fir forest. After walking 2.7 miles and gaining over 1,700-ft. the trail passes an old cow camp containing two wood structures.

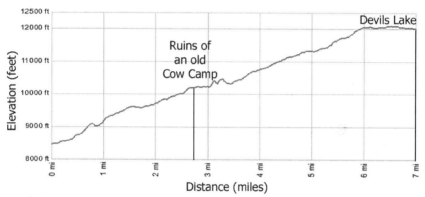

At the end of the road the trail curves to the southeast and travels along the base of a ridge through forest and meadows above the north side of Devil's Creek. Near the head if the drainage the path makes a wide arc to the northeast to avoid the talus clad slopes of the north facing escarpment of the Cannibal Plateau.

At 4.5 miles the trail briefly breaks out of the trees as it climbs through an area cleared by avalanche activity. Be sure to turn around and look west where you will see the tip of Uncompahgre Peak peeking above a ridge.

Soon the trail curves right (southeast) and ascends a wide gully between the Calf Creek Plateau (to the east) and Cannibal Plateau (to the west). At the 6 mile mark the grade abates. The final mile of the trail to Devil's Lake crosses open meadows dotted with small tarns. The lake lies nestled in a bowl/saddle between the Calf Creek and Cannibal Plateaus, surrounded by a huge meadow. Do not be surprise if you to run into large flocks of sheep grazing around the lake.

The Devil's Creek Trail can be used in conjunction with the Powderhorn Lakes Trail, the Powderhorn Park Trail, the Middle Fork Trail and the East Fork Trail for extended backpacking trips.

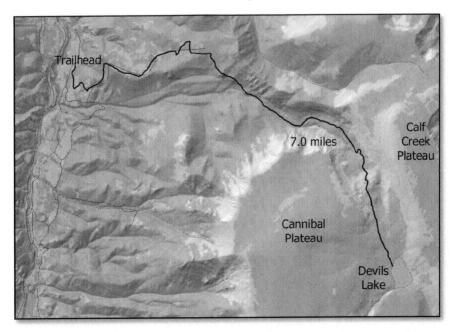

Driving Directions

Driving Directions From Lake City: From Lake City take Highway 149 north for 7 miles and turn right (east) on a dirt road heading northeast. A large brown sign marks the entrance to this road advising that the road is steep and narrow. Follow the road as it crosses a bridge spanning the Lake Fork River and heads up a hill to another dirt road to the left marked with a "TRAILHEADS" sign. Turn left onto this road and continue about 0.5 mile up the road to the Devil's Creek Trailhead. The gate at the bridge does not open to the public until June 15th.

35. Powderhorn Lakes ★★★★★
Distance: 9.6 miles (RT)

An interesting hike through forest and meadows to a scenic lake basin nestled beneath the eastern escarpment of the Calf Creek Plateau (12,644-ft.) in the Powderhorn Wilderness.

Distance: 7.8 - 9.6 miles (RT)
Elevation: 11,140-ft. at Trailhead
Maximum elevation: 11,870-ft.
Elevation Gain: 1,050-ft.
Difficulty: moderate

Basecamp: Lake City
Area: Powderhorn Wilderness, Gunnison BLM
Best Season: July - September
USGS Map(s): Powderhorn

Why Hike to Powderhorn Lakes

In the northern reaches of the San Juan Mountains lies the Powderhorn Wilderness, a rugged, glacier carved landscape consisting of large expanses of alpine tundra, spruce forests, and several alpine lakes at nearly 12,000-ft. The wilderness harbors two huge plateaus over 12,000-ft., the Cannibal Plateau and the Calf Creek Plateau, that make up the largest relatively flat expanse of alpine tundra in the lower 48 states. The plateaus were created by Tertiary volcanic deposits that are believed to be 5,000-ft. thick in some place.

The Powderhorn Lakes lay in the heart this incredible wilderness, in a huge glacial-chiseled cirque beneath the eastern side of the Calf Creek Plateau. The cirque's steep rock walls rise 450-ft. to 700-ft. from the lakeshores to the plateau.

An interesting trail travels through a diverse landscape of forests and meadows to the pretty lake basin. The lakes are set amid meadows surrounded by trees. The Powderhorn Lakes trails connects with other trails leading to the high plateaus and the Devil's Creek trail, offering opportunities for extended backpacking trips in the area.

Trailhead to Powderhorn Lakes

The path to the Powderhorn Lakes climbs southwest through a forest of Engelmann spruce along the eastern side of a long valley. At the head of the valley the trail crest a ridge and then drops into a large scenic wildflower-filled meadow at 1.5 miles. If you're lucky you may see elk grazing in the meadow in the early morning or late evening. Take a short side trip to the meadow's western rim for nice views to the northwest.

The trail descends gently across the meadow and then skirts its southwestern edge before reentering the trees at 1.9 miles. The trail, now in the West Fork of Powderhorn drainage, follows a rolling traverse, crossing a low ridge before dropping into minor drainage with a small lake set amid meadows filled with scrub willows.

Beyond the lake the trail returns to the trees, climbs a small rise and then loses 130-ft. in 0.2 miles. At the bottom of the drop the path turns southwest, paralleling the unseen West Fork of Powderhorn Creek. Another short, moderately steep climb leads to the top of a small hill at 3.4 miles and the junction with the trail to Hidden Lake, heading west.

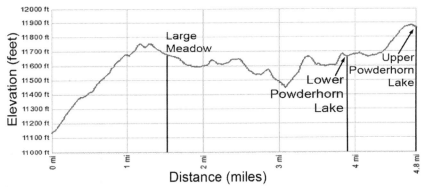

From the junction the path descends to and skirts the marshy meadows along the north side of the creek, passing several beaver ponds along the way and arrives at a trail junction with a sign pointing straight ahead to the Powderhorn Lakes. (The unsigned trail to the left is the Middle Fork Trail that climbs to the Calf Creek Plateau.)

Soon after the junction the trail ascends a small rise and arrives at Lower Powderhorn Lake at 3.9 miles. The lake sits at the eastern end of a large cirque. The cirque's steep rocky walls rise over 440-ft. above the lake to the Calf Creek Plateau.

To reach Upper Powderhorn Lake follow the trail as it skirts marshy meadows around the right (northwest) side of the lake. At the end of the lake the trail climbs a hillside through forest and meadows to the upper lake basin, gaining a little over 200-ft. in 0.6 miles.

Reach Upper Powderhorn Lake at 4.8 miles. The lake lies cradled in a glacier-carved bowl beneath the eastern escarpment of the Calf Creek Plateau. Steep volcanic rock walls rise 500-ft. to 700-ft. from the southern and western shoreline of the large lake to the plateau. Good campsites are located on the north and eastern sides of the lake.

The Powderhorn Lakes Trail can be used in conjunction with the East Fork Trail, the Middle Fork Trail and the Powderhorn Park Trail for a nice backpacking trip.

The Lower Powderhorn Lake provides fair to good trout

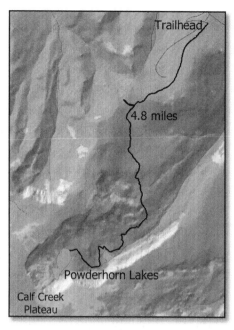

fishing as do the stream and beaver ponds of the West Fork of Powderhorn Creek. The Upper Powderhorn Lake sometimes has fish and sometimes suffers from winter kill.

Driving Directions

Driving Directions From Lake City: Drive north on Hwy 149 for just over 24 miles and turn right on Indian Creek Road / County Road 58. Follow the rough 2-wheel drive road for 10 miles. The trailhead sign and parking area are at the end of the road.

Driving Directions From Gunnison: Go 9 miles west on Hwy. 50 to Hwy.149 and turn left. Follow Hwy. 149 south for 20 miles. Turn left on Indian Creek Road (County Rd. 58) and follow the rough 2-wheel drive road for 10 miles. The trailhead sign and parking area are at the end of the road.

Appendix: Hiking Tips
Staying healthy and safe in the backcountry.

Hiking in the backcountry is a wonderful experience but can also be hazardous if you are not properly prepared. Here are some tips to help you to stay healthy and safe. For more backcountry hiking safety information check out the Hiking Safety tips from the American Hiking Society.

Trip Preparation

Your trip will be more enjoyable and safer if you take the time to plan it at home. Use forest recreation maps, topographic maps and trail guides to create an itinerary, calculate mileage and elevation gains, understand the terrain and learn about any potential hazards.

Take someone with you. Traveling with at least one hiking companion adds to your safety margin.

Before leaving home always leave your itinerary with a relative or friend. Write a full account of who is going, where you are going and when you will be back. For overnight trips include where you plan to stay each night.

Check current conditions posted on the forest service website to find out if there are any know hazards such as slippery roads, high fire danger and flash flood warnings. If possible, stop by the nearest Ranger Station before your trip to get the latest information.

Get in shape before the trip. Do not attempt a trip that is beyond your physical capabilities. Fatigue often leads to injuries.

What to Pack

Sudden shifts in weather are one of the backcountry's greatest dangers. Dress in layers and take the gear needed to keep you warm and dry if the weather turns for the worse. It may seem silly to carry a hat, gloves, rain gear (including pants) and a Polartec when starting your hike on a beautiful sunny day. But you will be glad you have carried all this gear if you get caught in high country during a ferocious afternoon thunderstorm with gale force wind, plummeting temperatures, hail and heavy rains.

I recommend that you bring a warm fleece or wool pullover, a waterproof jacket and pants, a hat, sunglasses, sunscreen, lip balm, insect repellant, first-aid kit, pocket knife, flashlight or headlamp, waterproof matches, maps, compass, a mirror and whistle for signaling if you are lost, plenty of water, and extra food. Wear sturdy boots that are broken in and are comfortable and know how they respond to wet slippery surfaces. A trekking pole or walking stick can be very helpful in maintaining your balance in hazardous conditions Take plenty of water and food. It's very important to drink water! See the section on dehydration under hazards.

Weather

Before you leave check the current weather forecast and change your plans if necessary.

Weather in the mountains is unpredictable. A beautiful sunny day can turn nasty in a blink of an eye. Keep an eye on the weather. High passes, exposed ridges, areas above the timberline, open meadows and isolated trees are dangerous places to be during a lightning storm. Respect Mother Nature and head downhill when you see storms approaching.

During July and August thunderstorms are most common in the afternoons. Your best bet is to get your butt out of bed early and plan your day so you are down from the high passes and ridges by early afternoon to avoid any potential bad weather.

Heavy rains can cause rivers and streams to rise rapidly. The stream you rock-hopped across on the way up the trail can become a raging torrent that becomes hazardous to cross. When in doubt, wait out the storm and let the rivers go down before trying to cross. Move to higher ground and avoid gullies and drainages.

Hazards

Giardia: Don't Drink the Water!!! Giardia, a microscopic organism that can cause severe diarrhea for up to two weeks, is widespread. You should assume all waterways are infected. The most effective treatment to make water safe to drink is to boil it. A good filter can also remove most harmful organisms present in mountain water. Choose a filter with a pore size less than 0.5 microns or a Steripen. These filters will effectively remove most harmful bacteria and protozoa (including Giardia) or, in the case of a Steripen, sterilize the water. Another option is to use iodine tablets to disinfect water collected on the hike. For short trips take a supply of water from home or other domestic sources.

Dehydration and Heat: Heat exhaustion and heat stroke can result from continued exposure to high temperatures and inadequate or unbalanced replacement of fluids. Adults require two quarts of water per day and four quarts or more for strenuous activity at high elevations. To maintain a high energy level and avoid dehydration by:

- Drink 8 to 16 ounces of water before hiking.
- Drink frequently when on the trail.
- Drink as much water as possible during lunch and throughout the evening.
- Limit caffeine drinks such as coffee or cola.
- Avoid alcoholic drinks.
- Plan ahead for drinking water. Don't allow water to run out before resupplying.
- Take breaks in the shade.

Prevent sunburn by wearing lightweight, light colored, and loose fitting clothing that allows air to circulate and sweat to evaporate while offering protection from direct sun. Bare skin absorbs the sun's radiant heat and raises body temperature. Understand the signs and symptoms of heat disorders including heat cramps, heat exhaustion and heat stroke.

Hypothermia: Hypothermia, caused by rapid loss of body heat, is the most dangerous illness of backcountry travel. Hypothermia can occur even in the warm summer months. Symptoms of hypothermia include: apathy, confusion, drowsiness, loss of coordination, pale or cold skin, uncontrollable shivering, shock, slurred speech, and weakness.

To prevent hypothermia, wear non-cotton clothing in layers, including a waterproof outer layer, that allow you to adjust to changing weather and temperatures. To treat hypothermia get the victim out of the wind and any wet clothing they may be wearing. Because skin-to-skin contact can quickly warm somebody back up again, place the victim in a dry sleeping bag then have one or two heat donors surround the victim. When fit for travel, carry or help the victim walk out and get medical attention as soon as possible.

Lightning: During a lightning storm avoid mountaintops, ridgelines, trees, rocks, and boulder fields. Go to a low-lying area and move away from others in your group. Turn off your electronic devices and remove any metal objects you are carrying including jewelry, watches, keys, knife, etc. Make your body a single point ground by putting your ankles and knees together and then crouching down. This posture lessens your chances of being a lightning rod or of a charge entering one foot from the ground, traveling through your vital organs, and exiting through your other foot. Do not lie flat on the ground because electrical current from a strike can easily travel through your vital organs this way, too. If your hair stands on end, immediately take the above safety precautions. A lightning strike could be eminent.

Altitude Sickness: Altitude sickness may occur if you overexert at high elevations (above 5,000 feet) where oxygen supply is reduced. Symptoms of high altitude sickness include nausea, dizziness, confusion, and fatigue. Before hiking at high altitudes it is best to acclimatize yourself by sleeping at these elevations a night or two. If you or someone in your party experiences high altitude sickness symptoms on a hike, do not go any higher! Descend as quickly as possible and, if symptoms get worse, get medical attention.

Fatigue: Exhaustion and fatigue occur because the person may be pushing too hard and is embarrassed to ask the group to slow down. A good principle of backcountry travel is take it slow, rest often, drink and eat snacks frequently to restore body energy and stay warm.

Fatigue slows your awareness and preparedness to hike safely. Watch out for other members of your party getting fatigued and take appropriate action and care.

Leave No Trace

Always practice Leave No Trace technique with hiking and backpacking. Please visit the Leave No Trace website to learn about the 7 Leave No Trace Principles.

Other Useful Tips

Hiking on Variable Terrain: Identify safe routes and local conditions. Test and use secure footing and never run down slopes. Step over logs, not on them. Know how to fall; protect your head and back and roll with the fall. Take extra precautions when encountering steep, loose, or wet trails.

Horses and Pack Stock: When you encounter travelers who have horses or pack stock, move off the trail on the downhill side and let them pass. Horses are easily frightened and have the right-of-way on trails.

Fall Hunting Season: We recommend that you don't hike alone during hunting season and that you stay on established trails. All hikers, as well their dogs, should wear at least one piece of florescent orange clothing during hunting season.

Bears: Bears are generally shy and will avoid people. If you should encounter a bear on the trail, back away slowly while facing the bear. Before you hike in Bear Country be sure to read Be Bear Aware, published by the Sierra National Forest.

Made in the USA
San Bernardino, CA
04 May 2017